This book belongs to

_____

...a girl after God's own heart.

A Girl After God's Own Heart

Devotional

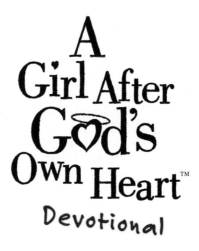

Elizabeth George

HARVEST HOUSE PUBLISHERS
EUGENE, OREGON

Material for devotions adapted from:

A Girl After God's Own Heart™ by Elizabeth George, Copyright © 2010

A Young Woman After God's Own Heart: A Devotional by Elizabeth George, Copyright © 2008

Cover by Garborg Design Works, Savage, Minnesota

HARVEST KIDS is a registered trademark of The Hawkins Children's LLC. Harvest House Publishers, Inc., is the exclusive licensee of the federally registered trademark HARVEST KIDS.

A GIRL AFTER GOD'S OWN HEART™ DEVOTIONAL
Copyright © 2012 by Elizabeth George
Published by Harvest House Publishers
Eugene, Oregon 97408
www.harvesthousepublishers.com

ISBN 978-0-7369-6685-6 (Milano Softone™)
ISBN 978-0-7369-4765-7 (padded HC)
ISBN 978-0-7369-4766-4 (eBook)

Printed in China

19 20 21 22 23 / RDS-SK / 9 8 7 6 5 4 3

Hi There!

I'm Elizabeth. And I want to welcome you to this cool little book of really great devotions written just for you. That's right! As I write books for girls, I think about you—where you live. What your family is like. What you look like. Whether or not you have braces. If you have a pet. How old you are. I even wonder about your favorite color, food, song, and hobby.

In other words, I have you in my heart and mind as I write to *you!*

Your journey with God is THE most important journey you will ever take. It's the trip of a lifetime. And the best thing about it? It leads you to God. God loves you. He loves you so much that He sent His precious and only Son, Jesus, to die for you on the cross so you could enjoy Him and live with Him forever.

That, my wonderful, super, beautiful-in-God's-eyes friend, is what the devotions in this book are all about. Just you...and your relationship with God.

So please, have some fun! Take a minute or two each day to learn more about Him and how much He treasures *you*. You are special to me. And you are special to your parents and grandparents. And you are oh-so-special to your heavenly Father!

> In His amazing and everlasting love,
> Your friend and sister in Christ,
>
> *Elizabeth George*

1

Being "In"

There's nothing wrong with being included as a part of a group of girls. In fact, having friends is an important part of your social life. But it *is* a problem if you're not focused on the most important thing—being "in" with God. He designed your life so that it works best when *He* is at the center of it. If you're not following God's heart, you're not going in the right direction.

You can still be team captain, know some cool girls, and have some good friends. But first make sure you're "in" with Jesus. Read your Bible. Pray. And pray for your friends. And be sure to ask Him if what you're doing makes Him happy. Then give Him all you've got!

Jesus, it's so easy to get caught up in caring about what others think that I forget to focus on You. Please let my friendship with You be the most important one in my life. I want to be "in" with You! Amen.

Attention, Please!

So many things—big and small—attract your attention and distract you from what's truly important. They can even turn your heart away from God and others and onto yourself instead.

Wouldn't you like to get better at paying attention to what *really* matters? Try this. When you wake up in the morning, remind yourself of your number one goal—becoming a girl after God's own heart. Then pray. Ask God to help you focus on the things He says are important. And then step into your brand new day with a happy heart.

Lord, sometimes it's hard to pay attention to You
when so many cool things and people and hobbies
are in my life. Please help me to remember to
focus on You, and what's important to You. Amen.

3

Treasure Hunt

Did you know that God has a treasure for those who choose to follow Him? Matthew 6:21 says, "Where your treasure is, there your heart will be also."

When it comes to treasure, you have a choice to make. You can choose to look for the things you want and think are important, or you can let God direct you to the treasure He has for you—a life of fabulous blessings especially for *you*.

What's really neat is that God's treasure isn't hidden. And it's not hard to find. As you go through each day and follow God's path, He will lead you step by step to discover the many treasures He has just for you along the way!

God, please help me to make Your treasure
my treasure, to focus the wants, dreams, and
desires of my heart on You. I want You to be
the most valuable prize in my life. Amen.

Adventure Story

Don't you just love the first day back in school after summer? That's the day everyone gets to share about their summer adventures. Probably your "adventures" weren't about sitting at home watching TV or playing computer games. They were maybe about an exciting camping trip, a fun hike, or even a visit to another state or country.

Well, God has a great adventure planned for you—a trip designed for you and you alone. If you decide to go, you'll have adventure after adventure. And you'll have lots of stories to share with others—stories of how God helped you every step of the way. How He showed you things about yourself you didn't know. How He blessed you, surprised you, gave you something special.

Be sure you share your stories with others. Maybe they will want to join you on your adventure into the Lord's great love, too!

Jesus, help me say yes to the adventures You have planned just for me. I might feel scared sometimes, but I know You will take care of me. And give me the courage to share my stories with others so they too can know about You. Amen.

No One Loves You More

Who loves you the most? Your friends? Nope. Your grandparents? Not quite. Your parents? Not them, either. As much as all these people love you, guess what? God loves you so much more! And becoming a girl after God's own heart starts by knowing—every day, deep down in your heart—that God loves you more than anyone else does.

The Bible tells you that...

- God is love (1 John 4:8), and

- God so loved the world (including you!) that He gave His one and only Son, that whoever believes in Him will not perish but have eternal life (John 3:16).

Jesus died so you could have a place in heaven forever with Him. No one *could* ever love you more. And no one *will* ever love you more!

> *Dear Lord, thank You for loving me. This is awesome...amazing...super cool! Help me remember that You love me more than anyone ever could. And help me remember to keep saying, "Thank You"! Amen.*

Follow the Leader

Isn't it fun to remember playing Follow the Leader with your friends? Maybe you've hopped on one foot, waddled like a duck, crawled like a baby, or did other silly things the leader asked everyone to do.

But hey, did you know that God wants you to play Follow the Leader with Him? In the Bible, Jesus lets us know how important it is to follow Him: "If you love me, you will obey what I command" (John 14:15).

How can you follow God's leading? Keep this thought in mind: "If God wants me to do something, I'm going to do it. And if God doesn't want me to do something, I'm not going to do it." As you follow Him, remember that He will always lead you to a place that is good! You can follow Him without any worries.

*Lord, thank You that I can follow You through
life. Please guide me and help me to live
as a girl who does what You want me to
do. Thank You for loving me...and leading
me in Your path—the right path. Amen.*

The Ultimate Answer Key

Life can sometimes be like taking a test. Sometimes you have to make choices, and it's hard to know what the right one is. Life would be so much easier if you could sneak a peek at an answer key from time to time, wouldn't it?

Well, guess what? You *do* have an answer key. In fact, you have the *ultimate* answer key. It's called the Bible, and it says, "Your word is a lamp to my feet and a light for my path" (Psalm 119:105).

Don't ever feel bad about checking God's answer key when you're in the middle of a tough problem. That's why He gave you the Bible!

God, thank You for giving me Your Word. It's my own personal guide to help me know what You want me to do. When I'm stuck, please help me remember to look in my Bible. Thank You that Your answers are always right! Amen.

Read All About It!

I hope your favorite book is my favorite book. It's a book filled with true stories, written especially for you. My favorite book is the Bible, and I make sure I read it every day. I hope you read your Bible every day, too.

Maybe sometimes you don't read the Bible because you have trouble understanding some of the words and stories. Please don't let this discourage you. God has put people in your life who can help you understand His Word—such as your parents, grandparents, a Sunday school teacher, your youth group leader, or even your favorite church camp counselor. If you can't think of anyone to talk to, start praying. Ask God to bring someone who can help you understand His Word better. He wants you to know His Word too, so He'll do it!

God, I love You and I love Your Word.
I want to know what it says...and what it
means. Please help me to understand it. And
help me to live by this verse: "I have hidden
your word in my heart that I might not sin
against you" (Psalm 119:11). Amen.

Your "Things I Love" List

If you made a list of "Things I Love," what would be on it? Your parents, I hope! And your siblings and pets if you have those. Probably a best friend...or two or three. And some of your favorite activities—swimming, soccer, drawing. Maybe even some yummy foods like ice cream or chocolate!

And don't forget God. He loves you dearly. You are His special treasure. You're on His "Things I Love" list! And guess what? He really wants you to love *Him*. In fact, He wants to be at the very top of your "Things I Love" list. He wants you to love Him more than all other things. In the Bible we read, "Love the Lord your God with all your heart and with all your soul and with all your mind" (Matthew 22:37).

Now *that's* a lot of love. But trust me—Jesus is worth it!

> *Lord, I want You to be right at the tippy-top of*
> *my "Things I Love" list. You should be there...*
> *forever. Thank You for loving me, and for giving*
> *so many wonderful things to love. I truly want*
> *to love You with all my heart, all my soul, and*
> *all my mind—every single day! Amen.*

The Best Choice

Okay, so you've decided that you're going to love God more than anything else in your life. Woohoo—high five! But *how* do you do this? It's easy. You start fresh each day. Every morning you choose to put Jesus first in your life and your heart. Here are my favorite ways to do this:

- When you go to bed at night, tell God you love Him and you'll think about Him first thing as soon as you wake up. Then say, "Good night, Lord. I love You!"

- When you wake up, say, "Good morning!" to God. Thank Him for His love, His blessings, and all the good things in your life.

When you make the choice to love the Lord more than anything else, you're making the best choice of all!

Jesus, I can't say it enough! Thank You for loving me. I want to love You back and put You first each and every day—when I get up in the morning, when I go to bed at night, and all the times in between. I want to choose You, to be Your girl after God's own heart, all day, every day! Amen.

11

Write It Down

When I was a young girl, I dearly loved writing in my diary. It was a special, private place where I could share my thoughts and share about what was happening in my life. I didn't want to forget these things, so I wrote them down.

I want to encourage you to keep a diary or journal too, if you don't already. You can write about friends, activities, and school. But most important of all, you can write what you are learning about Jesus. You can try to put on paper how much you love Him. And you can write down your prayers—and see how He answers.

Give it a try! Make the words in your diary or journal personal ones, the kind that come straight out of your heart. They are just between you and God. You'll love watching the story of a wonderful friendship with Jesus grow stronger and stronger.

Lord, so much happens to me each day. And
I learn so much about You! As I begin to write
it all down, I pray it will become a love story, a
record of my growing friendship with You. Amen.

Take Your Temperature

What does your mom do when you're sick? I'm guessing she probably asks about how you're feeling. She may try to get you to lie down and rest. And she may even take your temperature so she can find out if you're just a little bit sick or *really* sick!

Did you know that your heart has a temperature too? The Bible talks about three heart temperatures:

- *A cold heart* doesn't even think about God—at all!
- *A lukewarm heart* is bored with God.
- *A hot heart* is the kind of heart God wants you to have, which boils over with excitement and love for Him.

So get ready to turn up the heat of your heart temperature as you grow to love Him more and grow in your commitment to Him!

God, help me turn up the temperature
of my heart so that it's sky-high for You!
May I experience the incredible blessings
of a heart on fire for You. Amen.

Warm Up Your Heart

Again and again in this devotional you will read about God's great love for you. There's a reason for this—it's the whole reason God created you! He wants to have a relationship with you and give you eternal life. Just think about how much He loved you before you ever loved Him. Amazing, isn't it?

I hope your heart is as excited about Jesus right now as mine is! And it's always a good thing to pray that your heart will warm up even more and burn hot with a real love for Him.

You can pray right now. Tell God that you want to know more about the Lord, that you want to love Him more and more. It's the most important prayer you could ever say—a prayer to warm up your heart. It is my prayer that you will spend each day thanking God for His love and wanting to follow His plan for your life.

Jesus, help me to love You more, to know You better, and to follow You with all my heart. I want to run a temperature that's sky-high for You. I want to live life with joy and excitement, knowing that I am secure in Your love. Amen.

14

Living It Out

We've chatted a lot about the importance of having your heart focused on Christ, about living as a girl after God's own heart. Now it's time to turn to the nitty-gritty of living it out. And this can be really fun...but it can also be really hard!

A good place to start living out God's plan is at home, beginning with your very own room. Whether you have your own space or you share it, it's important for you to take good care of the room.

Think about all that your mom does in your home—she cleans it, decorates it, cares for it. Look at what she does, and let her be your role model. Your space doesn't have to be perfect. But you do want to keep it nice and neat. For sure you'll want to have your friends see your space. This will also help you learn how to take care of everything God gives you in the future!

Lord, help me to appreciate what You and others
like my mom have done for me. And help me
take care of what You've given me. I want to
grow as a girl after Your heart in every area
of my life—beginning with my room! Amen.

15

Take Care!

Did you know that *God* wants you to clean your room? And no, your parents didn't tell me to write this down! Taking care of your space is an important part of following God and doing what He wants you to do. The Bible says, "Whatever you do, work at it with all your heart, as working for the Lord, not for men" (Colossians 3:23).

As a growing girl, God expects you to take care of the things that belong to you—your clothes, your bed, your desk. Taking care of your space shows good character. It proves that you can set a goal and then work to achieve it. That you care about your things.

Remember, God wants you to do your best in every area of your life—even when it comes to taking care of your room.

Jesus, thank You for the gift of my own space and a place to call home. I know that You have given me all things, and that it's my responsibility to take care of them. Please help me to do my chores well...and with a happy heart. Amen.

Reflection of Your Heart

Think about your room and what makes it so special—the posters or pictures you have on your walls, the decorations on your desk or nightstand, your books and magazines. The things you have in your room are a reflection of who you are, and other people can get a very good idea of what you're like just by looking at what you have chosen to display.

Now is a good time to ask yourself, *Do the things in my room bring honor to God?* Or, here's another way to look at it. Suppose Jesus were to stop in to visit and see your space. Is there anything you would want to hide before He got there? If so, it probably shouldn't be there! It should go—now!

Your space is indeed special. Be sure to thank God for a warm place to sleep, nice clothes to wear, and pretty little treasures that make you happy. Colossians 3:15 tells us to "be thankful" for God's gifts to us!

> *Jesus, please help me to remember that what's in my room is a reflection of my heart. Let my space be a place that brings honor and glory to You, a place that shows I'm a girl after Your own heart. Amen.*

Choosing Wisely

How did you spend your time today? Did you play with a friend? Watch TV? Do a craft project? Text your friends? Go on a bike ride? Did you take any time to pick up your room and help your family around the house? I hope so!

Although doing housework might not be as fun as a bike ride or beading bracelets, God does ask you to help take care of the place where you live. The Bible says a woman after God's heart, whether she's a young woman or older, "watches carefully all that goes on throughout her household, and is never lazy" (Proverbs 31:27 TLB).

This powerful verse describes the actions of a wise woman—and a wise girl. She takes care of her stuff—and she isn't lazy! So do pay attention to picking up after yourself and spending your time wisely. God wants you to make wise choices!

Jesus, sometimes it's so hard to stop and decide to keep my room clean and pick up after myself. But I realize You want me to learn to use my time well and not be lazy. Thank You for growing me up to be a wise girl so that someday I can become a wise woman! Amen.

Neat Freak = Jesus Freak

You've probably heard the term *Jesus Freak*. It's used to speak of someone who's totally into Jesus and living her life for Him. She's sold out to Jesus and on fire for Him. What a great thing! But did you know that being a neat freak can also help you become more of a Jesus Freak? What?!

Just think about this: Your room is *you*. If it's neat and tidy, that tells people something about your character, about who you are on the inside. And if your room is an absolute mess, people are going to get some definite ideas about you!

So make sure you vacuum *your* floor, dust *your* furniture, put away *your* clothes, organize *your* books and papers, and clean *your* desk. (Did you notice my emphasis on a certain word?) Begin living out *your* love for God by being a neat freak—and enjoy the results!

God, I know You want me to keep my room tidy
and inviting and to be responsible with my chores.
Help me to remember Your wishes as
I work to be a neat freak who loves Jesus. Amen.

Bonding God's Way

Do you love looking through magazines and catalogs that show beautiful dream rooms? Oh wow! It's so much fun to get some new ideas for your space, but be sure you include your mom in your thinking. Working together with mom makes things so much more enjoyable as the two of you share and plan and dream together.

And remember, as you share, there are good reasons why your mom might say yes or no to your ideas. Some things might be too expensive. Posters and pictures need to be hung carefully so they don't damage the walls. And the decor of your room needs to go with the rest of the house.

Titus 2:4-5 says, "The younger women...[are to be taught] to be busy at home." So ask your mom for her input. Go through magazines and catalogs, and start a "dream room" notebook. What a fun way to bond—*God's* way!

Lord, thank You that You have made me a unique person who likes to express herself in a certain way. And help me to appreciate my mom's advice. I know You have placed her in my life to love me and guide me. Amen.

Working It Out

Imagine how big the universe is—sun, moon, planets, and especially the distant stars! Makes you feel pretty small and insignificant, doesn't it? But you should never feel like you don't matter. God cares about you and is interested in every little detail of your life—like the pictures, books, and clothes in your room. And He wants to make sure that you are growing as a girl after His own heart.

When you're cleaning your desk or folding your clothes or making your bed, you can pray, listen to praise music, and talk to Jesus. You can even get together with a friend and help clean each other's rooms while you talk about what the Lord is doing in your lives. God created work to be fun and rewarding. What an awesome plan!

God, thank You for the opportunity to do chores—and for the creativity You have given me to make them more fun. When I look at my neat and shiny room, I'm reminded of the state of my heart—a heart that loves You. Amen.

21

Too Busy

Have you ever had a day when you felt like your parents were too busy for you? That it seemed like nobody had time to help you with your homework or talk with you about your problems with a friend at school? It's hard to go through a day like this!

This is when you have to remember that maybe your parents are working long hours to meet deadlines. That your brother or sister is super busy right now, so there isn't as much time left over for you. Whatever may be happening, do know that in the meantime—actually, *all* of the time!—you can turn to God with your concerns and worries. He's always there to listen to you! And He loves listening to you.

As you know, life gets tough sometimes. And it's easy to get busy. So pray for your parents and tell God how you're feeling. And don't ever forget that next to God, you are what's most important to your parents. So take a few minutes to pray. Then trust God to work things out.

Lord, please help me not to be sad when I feel
like I don't matter. That's just not true. When I
feel like this, help me to remember I can always
turn to You. You are never too busy. Amen.

No Put-downs

My mom is so stupid!" "What does my dad know, anyway?" Have you ever heard things like this said at school or in the neighborhood? Sadly, a lot of kids make these comments. And if you listen to too much of this kind of talk, you'll start thinking it's okay to talk about your parents this way, too.

Be careful! In the Bible, God says you are to honor your parents and that they are a special gift from Him to you. God gave you the parents He knew would be just right for you.

God loves families. His perfect plan is for them to live together in harmony, encouraging each other and building each other up. So instead of seeing your mom and dad as goofy, old-fashioned, or too strict, start seeing them as special gifts from God...just for you.

Jesus, thank You for my parents. Help me
not to make fun of or put down my parents
in front of my friends. Instead, let me speak
words of kindness about them. Let me tell
the world how great they are. Amen.

Keep Saying Thanks

Prayer is the best habit you can develop in your whole life! No matter where you are or what's happening around you, you can always talk to God. And it doesn't matter if you talk to Him out loud, in the quiet of your heart, or on paper. God cares a lot about you, and He loves to hear your prayers.

So try to pray every day. A good place to start is by praying for your mom and dad. When you do this, you become closer to them and start loving them more and more. And when you talk to God about your parents, thank Him for them: "Always [give] thanks to God the Father for everything" (Ephesians 5:20).

It's good to pray about things you're struggling with. But never forget that an important part of prayer is giving thanks to God. Thank Him now for your parents!

God, I know You want me to give thanks to You
for everything. So thank You for my parents.
Help me to listen to them, obey them, and
most of all, to love them even more! Amen.

The Importance of Saying "Thank You"

Two small words can really make a person's day—
thank you! When you take time to thank people,
you're letting them know that you notice and appreciate what they've done for you.

Your parents deserve your thank yous. For instance,
if they buy you new clothes, tell them thank you. If you
attend ballet or gymnastics classes or play on a sports
team, thank them for the time they spend driving you
to practice and for the money they pay and the volun-
teering they do. When you eat a meal, thank the person who cooked it. And when clean clothes "magically"
show up in your room, say thank you.

A wonderful bedtime ritual is to thank your parents for all they've done for you. Then you can thank
God for His blessings upon your family.

Jesus, open my eyes. Help me notice and
appreciate what my parents have done for
me. Help me grow a grateful heart. Most of
all, thank You for all You do for me—and
my family—every day. Thank You! Amen.

Ask for Advice

Are you facing friendship troubles? Is your school-work stumping you? Are you not sure whether to give up a sport or stick with it? With so much on your mind, it's hard to figure out the right thing to do!

Well, here's some super news! You can always turn to Jesus and the Bible for excellent advice. And more good news? God has also put people in your life who can help you make good decisions. He's given you teachers, youth leaders, and grandparents to help guide you. Best of all, you have your parents, who love you and want you to be happy. They can give you great advice and steer you in the right direction. And they have excellent wisdom to share. (Yes, they were once kids, too!) How wonderful to have a loving God *and* loving parents to go to for advice! Your assignment? Just ask.

Jesus, thank You that I don't have to face my troubles alone. Thank You that You always know what is best for me. Whew! And lead me to those who can help me make good decisions. Amen.

Do the Right Thing

When I was a girl, I loved going to slumber parties. One time, however, my parents said no to a certain slumber party. I was soooo upset because I was really looking forward to being a part of the excitement—and this group of girls! So what did I do? I'm ashamed to admit that I cried. I whined. I begged. And I even thought horrible things about my parents.

But do you know what happened? A bunch of boys showed up at the party that night, and the kids got so loud that the neighbors called the police. After I heard about what had happened, I was so thankful my parents had refused to let me go!

So remember—once your parents make a rule or a decision, it's important that you do what they say. When you honor God and your parents, God will reward you in a special way.

Lord, when my friends are doing things I can't
do, I sometimes feel upset with my parents.
Please help me to accept their wisdom and
their decisions with an obedient heart. Amen.

Talk About It

While it's important to obey your parents and respect their decisions, it's also okay to ask questions—in a calm, sweet way—about the things you don't agree upon. This will help you as you grow older. By talking with your parents now about choices and their possible consequences, you'll be better prepared to make good choices and honor God through your own decisions.

The key here is having a right attitude. For instance, never approach your parents in order to get your own way, and then pout or get angry if that doesn't happen. You can, however, ask (again, calmly and sweetly) the reasons for their decision. Maybe you can even ask what you can do to earn a privilege.

Proverbs 1:8 says, "Listen, my [child], to your father's instruction and do not forsake your mother's teaching." Listen carefully, do what your parents say, and, as always, do it with a happy heart.

God, I want to learn how to make choices that honor You and my parents. Help me hear Your heart so I can accept my parents' decisions with an open and happy heart. Amen.

Honor and Respect

Let's spend a minute talking about your teacher at school, or your sports coach, or your art instructor. When they ask you to do something, you probably do it, right? And you surely don't argue with them!

Now, let's switch to the home front. God has given you your parents as the ultimate teachers, coaches, and instructors in your life. So you should show just as much respect—more, in fact!—to them as you would to anyone else. Jesus has a pretty straightforward command on this one: "Honor your father and mother" (Matthew 15:4).

So be sure to give parents—and teachers, coaches, and instructors—the honor they deserve. That's what a girl after God's own heart does. Listen to them. Respect them. Submit to their authority. And the best thing is that by showing them honor, you also honor the Lord!

Jesus, thank You for the people in my life who are teaching me to be a better person. Thank You especially for my parents. Bless them, and help me to show them proper honor and respect. Amen.

One of Ten

Think about Matthew 15:4: "Honor your father and mother." Just five words—but powerful words! This is not just a suggestion from God, it's a *commandment*. And it's one of the Ten Commandments. That makes it a very important rule to follow, doesn't it?

So what does it mean to respect your parents? You are to treat them politely and with honor. You are to look for the good in them. You are to listen when they talk, accept their decisions, and seek to please them.

If you think about it, your relationship with your parents should look a lot like your relationship with God. God—like your parents—loves you and cares about you. In return, you love and honor Him. That's how it works best!

Lord, You have asked me to honor my parents, and I want to obey You. Thank You for giving me rules like this one to help me know how to live right. Amen.

Rewards for Obedience

You have a mind of your own. You know what you like and what you don't. You also know what makes you happy. And you have definite ideas and preferences because you're one-of-a-kind!

While it's fantastic to be your own unique person, you can't go through life doing whatever you please. First you need to make sure what you want to do is the *right* thing to do. You do this by asking for advice from God, your parents, or another older and wiser person—and then obeying that advice. As Ephesians 6:1 says, "Children, obey your parents in the Lord, for this is right."

There's that connection again—parents and obedience! It's important because God says it so many times! God designed the parent-child relationship to be the best kind of relationship of all. So seek your parents' approval and God's approval, and you can't go wrong.

God, help me to ask for advice and get
approval from my parents for the things
I do and the choices I make. Thank You
for loving parents to guide me! Amen.

Don't Be Foolish

Of course you know how special you are to God and how very much He loves you. But He does have some pretty strong warnings and words about bad behavior. In Proverbs 15:20 He says, "A foolish [person] despises his mother." You don't want to be a foolish girl! That isn't God's plan for you at all.

To *despise* someone means to mock them and to have no respect for them. This is the opposite of God's command to honor your parents—as well as others. So be careful not to speak badly or make fun of anyone—especially someone you love, respect, and honor, and super-especially your parents.

When you feel like saying something mean, stop yourself. Take a deep breath and then either say something sweet and positive...or don't say anything at all. Then pray about your heart. Ask God to turn your thoughts from foolish to loving and wise.

Jesus, I don't want to disobey and disappoint
You. When I'm tempted to speak words that
are unkind or not true, turn my thoughts
toward You and all that is good. Amen.

32

Trust

Have you ever done a "trust fall"? A group of people stand behind you, and as you fall backward, they catch you and keep you from hitting the ground. This doesn't sound that hard, but it is! You can't see the people behind you, and you can only hope that they really will catch you! That's trust.

Trusting others can be a challenge, but we can always trust God. The Bible says, "Trust in the LORD with all your heart and lean not on your own understanding; in all your ways acknowledge him, and he will make your paths straight" (Proverbs 3:5-6).

Wow—what a promise! As you live out each day becoming a girl after God's own heart, trust that God is leading and growing you. When you trust God, He will always catch you, no matter what happens.

Lord, it can be hard to trust when I don't know what's going to happen. Keep me focused on following You and the path You want me to take. Thank You for always being there to catch me! Amen.

Showing Love

How many ways can you think of to say, "I love you"? Well, you can say the words, and that's a good thing! But did you know there are many other ways to show your love? When you help your mom with dinner—especially without being asked—you're saying *I love you*. When you spend hours making a birthday card for a close friend, you're saying *I love you*. When you read your little brother his favorite picture book for the hundredth time, you're saying *I love you*.

First John 3:18 says, "Dear children, let us not love with words or tongue but with actions and in truth." So love isn't just the words you say. It's also what you do and your behavior. By showing your love for others—saying it *and* living it—you're also showing your love for God. Isn't that awesome?

Jesus, I love You. I want to share my love
for You and others through my words
and deeds. Help me find new ways I
can show my love every day. Amen.

34

That Hurts!

I'm sure you've hurt someone without meaning to, right? Maybe you were in a grumpy mood, and when your dad asked you to unload the dishwasher, you lashed out in anger. Or maybe someone was mean to you in dance class, so you came home and said unkind things about her to your sister. Before you knew it, you were upset with everyone and everything!

What is it about hurting others that makes it so... well...hurtful? When we hurt others, we also hurt ourselves. Even worse, we hurt God. It saddens His heart when we are unkind and disobedient.

So how can you make things right? First, pray and ask God for help. Then go to the people you've hurt and apologize. Finally—and this is really important— stay connected to God. Let Him teach you about love.

Jesus, I'm so sorry for the times I've hurt others. Thank You that I can make things right by praying and asking for forgiveness. Keep me connected to You! Amen.

Change of Heart

What do you do with your clothes when you spill food on them or get them all sweaty or muddy? You change them! And what about your heart? Though you can't spill food on it, your heart can get sweaty or muddy or soiled, so to speak.

The theme verse for becoming a girl after God's own heart is Acts 13:22. In this verse, God describes the heart of the man He chose to be king over His people: "I have found David...a man after my own heart; he will do everything I want him to do."

Are you doing *everything* God wants you to do? If not, tell God you're sorry and ask for His help. Tell Him you want to love, honor, and obey Him by following His Word and doing everything He wants you to do. Then make the changes you need to make. And then...notice the difference!

Lord, I need a change of heart! I know I've said and done things that have made my heart icky. I want my heart to be clean and fresh for You. Thank You for Your forgiveness. Please give me a happy, obedient heart. Amen.

Sibling Stuff

You know the story of Cinderella, right? There's the nice, kind sister who does everything perfectly. Then there are the nasty, wicked stepsisters who...well, you know who they are and what they did! If you have siblings, you probably feel a bit like Cinderella at times. No matter what you do, there are days when you just don't get along!

Of course, at the end of the story Cinderella discovers that she's really a princess. And that's what you are, too—God's princess! And your sisters? Princesses as well! Brothers? Well, it might be hard to believe, but you guessed it—they're God's princes!

This may sound a little silly. But keep reminding yourself of this—especially on those days when you feel like you could never, *ever* be friends with your siblings. You're all part of God's royal family!

Lord, some days I really do feel like Cinderella.
I just can't get along with my brother
or sister. Help me see them as You do.
Focus my heart on You and my role as
a princess in Your kingdom. Amen.

Family Is First

Over the years your friends will come and go. But you will always have your family. While it might not seem like it right now, the day *will* come when you and your brothers and sisters will get along great with each other. That's why it's important to put your family first—before your friends, activities, and hobbies.

What can you do about extra activities? And how can you make sure you have enough time with your family? Ask your parents, and then let their decision on your activities be final. They know what is best for you and your family. So give it to God. Maybe something else will come along—something even better. Let God use your downtime at home to strengthen your family ties and relationships. Ask God to help you do your part toward having a great family.

God, I need to respect the decisions my
parents make about family time. Help
me to joyfully participate as a member
of the family You've given me. Amen.

Be Loyal

Next to Jesus and your friendship with Him, your family is your number one priority. One way you make them first is by showing love and support for your family members. You can cheer on your little brother in his soccer or T-ball games. You can attend your big sister's swim meets or piano recitals. You can even make signs for your dad's softball games or volunteer to help your mom set up for her Sunday school class.

After the game or activity, don't forget to tell them what a great job they did. Or, if they didn't get to play or it didn't go so well, you can give them a hug and say, "I'm so proud of you. Your day will come."

Be a loyal, giving, loving, and helpful family member. Be supportive in as many ways as you can!

Dear Lord, I have such a fun, unique family. Thank You for our similarities—and our differences! Help me to be a great sister and daughter who is there to support every member of my family in their efforts. Amen.

At All Times

A friend loves at all times and a brother is born for adversity" (Proverbs 17:17). Now read this verse again and insert the word *sister* where you see the words *friend* and *brother*. What does it mean?

Well, *you* are the sister who loves at all times (yes, *all* is correct!) and is "born for adversity." This means you have an important part to play in the lives of your family members—especially when they are feeling down or things aren't going so well. When someone in your family is hurting, Jesus wants you to be there for them.

God wants you to be a girl after His own heart. And what does this girl do? She loves her family members at *all* times—when things are going great as well as when times are rough. He created you to play an important role in your family. So turn on the love and support...at all times.

Lord, You have faith that I can show
kindness and love at all times. Give me
the words to say and the actions to do to
prove my love for my family. Amen.

Pray for Others

Think about this. The best way you can learn to love others is to pray for them. It might be a little hard to understand at first, but praying for others changes your heart. It's easy to fight with your siblings. It's easy to talk back to your parents. And it's easy to make fun of someone behind her back. But praying for others can be hard—especially if your feelings have been hurt, or you've been ignored or treated badly.

Jesus said, "I tell you, love your enemies and pray for those who persecute you" (Matthew 5:44). Crazy stuff! But did you know that you can't pray for someone and hate them at the same time? As you keep praying, you'll discover your feelings toward that person changing and turning from bad to good. That's what God can do in the heart of a girl who follows Him and prays for others!

Lord, it's so hard to show kindness to people who aren't nice to me. Help me with my thoughts. And help me with my prayers. Build up Your love in my heart so it's easy for me to love others. Amen.

Tame Your Tongue

It's no fun finding yourself on the receiving end of jokes, teasing, and name-calling. Even if the words are meant as a joke, they still hurt—a lot! And even though you can't control what others say or do, you are totally in control of what *you* say and do! You can choose to make fun of others—or not. You can decide to laugh at people and put them down—or not. You can choose to tame your tongue—or let it go.

You can't force someone else to be nice to you or to other people. But you *can* make things better by being nice yourself. God says, "Do not let any unwholesome talk come out of your mouths, but only what is helpful for building others up" (Ephesians 4:29). Choose to speak words that are good and true. When you do, you add more of God's love and joy into the world. And, hey, others might just start doing the same thing!

Jesus, when someone laughs at me or makes a joke about me, I confess, sometimes I want to be mean in return. Fill my heart with Your brand of love and kindness. Help me respond in the right way—Your way. Amen.

Make a Change

One of the scariest stories in the Bible is about what happened with two brothers, Cain and Abel. Do you know them? Cain was super mad at his brother because God preferred Abel's gift offering to Cain's. God spoke to Cain about his bad attitude in Genesis 4:6-7, saying, "Why are you angry?...sin is crouching at your door; it desires to have you, but you must master it."

If you know the end of this story, you know what Cain should have done. He should have made a change—a big change in his attitude toward his brother. And he could have prayed to God to take away his anger. Instead, "Cain attacked his brother Abel and killed him" (verse 8).

God has a message for you here. The next time you get mad at a brother or sister or friend, don't let your anger get out of control. Make a change in your bad attitude before it changes you!

Dear Lord, when I get angry with someone, please help me turn to You and ask for a change of heart. Give me the strength to master my sin. Amen.

You Love First

Here's a question for you. Should you only love someone if they first show love to you? The answer? No way! The Bible says, "A new command I give you: Love one another. As I have loved you, so you must love one another" (John 13:34). God is pretty clear that "one another" means *everyone*. It means loving your big sister...even when she calls you a brat. It means loving your little brother...even when he scatters your beads all around your room. It means loving your best friend...even when she lets you down.

It's hard to love when you don't feel like it or your feelings are hurt. But this is the kind of love God wants you to have—a love that comes from God's love for you and in you. He wants you to love first—and love always, no matter what. Love like this is a big challenge. Good thing you have a God who specializes in helping you with the big challenges!

Lord, I know You love me in spite of the bad things I say and do. Help me to know You love me and to love others with the same kind of love—especially when I don't feel like it. Amen.

Take Control

Don't you love that amazing sensation you get on a thrilling roller coaster? It's a blast of adrenaline. The anticipation builds as you wait in line. Then after you hop in and strap in, off you go! You're totally *not* in control of the ride—and that's what you love about it! Oh, yeah!

Life can be a lot like a roller coaster—especially as you grow up and experience changes in your body, your emotions, and your whole world. Sometimes those things make it seem as if your life is like a roller coaster! That's why you need to watch over your attitude. If you don't, you might hurt someone else big time—as well as yourself. So when your world seems to be racing out of control, remember Ephesians 4:32: "Be kind and compassionate to one another, forgiving each other, just as in Christ God forgave you." Then buckle in...and enjoy the ride!

Jesus, roller coasters are a ton of fun. But when my life turns into a roller coaster, I want off! Help me choose to show kindness and compassion to others, especially when life gets rough. Amen.

"All for One and One for All"

Does your family have a motto—words that you live by when the going gets tough? If not, here's a good one from the Three Musketeers—"All for one and one for all." In other words, be there for each other—think of each other, encourage each other, love each other.

How can you start doing this? Write a note of thanks to your big brother for the cool things he teaches you, and slip it under his door. Get involved in your little sister's life, playing dolls and stuffed animals with her...again! Learn to cook some simple meals with your mom or be your dad's number one helper around the house. You won't believe the difference little things like these can make!

A girl after God's own heart is also a big sister, or a little sister, or a daughter after God's own heart. Start living for your family today—all for one and one for all!

God, help me get my eyes off of my own life and on to the lives of my brothers, sisters, and parents. Let me be a part of making our home a better place as we all live for each other—especially as we live for You! Amen.

When You're an Only Child

We've talked quite a bit about families and how God wants you to treat your brothers and sisters. But what if you're an only child without any siblings? Do you get to skip over all you've read about getting along with brothers and sisters? Well, no!

Even if you don't have any siblings, you do have family members, friends, and lots of others you should get along with. So any advice about how to treat your siblings—like being kind to them, putting their needs first, being there for them—also applies to your cousins, friends, and everyone else.

So make sure you don't get so caught up in your own world that you forget to think of other people. Start imagining them as part of one big, happy family—a family you can love and serve!

God, even though I don't have brothers and sisters, I can still put Your advice about siblings into practice. Help me to see other people as part of my "bigger family" and to show kindness and care to them. Amen.

The Hard Stuff

Believe it or not, it is possible to feel like two different people. One part of you inhales books and loves writing. So you love English class! Another part of you can't seem to make sense of science—how things work, and experiments that never quite come out right. Or maybe you're great at math but not reading. Or you enjoy running and swimming, but not any sport involving a ball.

God made everyone different, with a variety of strengths and challenges. Nothing comes easily to us. But please don't give up—there are important lessons God wants you to learn from the hard stuff. And the hard stuff is where you can learn and grow the most! So thank God for the challenges you face. Dig a little deeper, and ask Him to help you accomplish what you can't do on your own.

Jesus, some things in life come easily to me, but other things seem impossible! Give me the determination to stick with the hard stuff. And please don't let me be too proud to ask for help—especially from You. Amen.

Growing Up

Oh, how I looked forward to growing up when I was a young girl! With each birthday came the opening of new doors—activities and privileges I was *finally* old enough for! And receiving all those presents was terrific, too—more treats and treasures that signified the passing of time and what a young lady I was becoming.

But if you are like me, you know that with each new year and birthday comes more responsibilities—an increase in chores, more difficult schoolwork, greater expectations about my behavior. Yes, life becomes more exciting...but it also becomes more challenging.

Thankfully, God never asks you to do more than you can handle. As you are growing up, you can turn to Him and ask Him to help you through your challenges. And then walk confidently through that newly opened door! That's how you become a young woman after God's own heart.

Jesus, most of the time growing up is great. But sometimes it can be hard, especially when I don't feel ready for that next thing coming. Please guide my steps and strengthen my heart. Amen.

Training for Life

No matter where you go to school—public school, private school, or home school—you can think of your classes as a training ground for life.

For starters, they help you develop good "people skills." School requires you to get along with a wide range of people—teachers, principals, classmates, friends, and new kids. Even if you're homeschooled, you probably take classes in a setting or a co-op with people who span a wide range of ages and abilities. In school, you also learn how to ask and answer questions, search for information, give reports, and share with others—all very important people skills!

God wants to use your terrific people skills to His glory as He grows you up as a girl after His own heart. So work hard to develop them!

Jesus, thank You that You are using school to teach me some really great skills. Help me as I spend time with others and grow as a girl after God's own heart. Amen.

Pay Attention

If someone followed you around school for one entire day and observed how you acted toward your teachers, friends, and other students, what would they see? Would they see a girl who respects authority, treats others with kindness, and thinks before she speaks and is careful about how she acts? Or would they see something else? Uh oh!

You already know it's not possible to always be perfect. Sometimes your emotions get the better of you, and you say things you later regret. And then there are those days when you have so much energy that sitting still is the last thing you want to do!

Yet school is an opportunity for you to show others what God can do in someone's life. Focus on what you need to be doing *right this moment*. And pray that Jesus will show you how to live for Him.

God, I really want to live for You. Help me to focus my energy on doing what's right. I want to make good choices so others can see what a difference You can make in a person's life. Amen.

Wealth and Wisdom

Imagine winning a shopping trip to your favorite store—with no limit on how much you can spend. Yahoo! You could bring home bags and bags of the most amazing things, and even buy a bunch of stuff for your friends. It's fun to dream about a shopping trip like this, isn't it? But did you know that you already have all the treasure your heart could possibly desire? God says so, right in His Word: "If you look for [wisdom] as for silver and search for it as for hidden treasure, then you will understand the fear of the LORD and find the knowledge of God" (Proverbs 2:4-5).

God's wisdom is wealth. And it's worth far more than the treasures in your favorite store. And you don't have to win a contest to receive it! God's promises are for real, and He gives freely. That's better than anything you could win in this world!

Jesus, I want to have Your wisdom and
the knowledge of You in my life. Help
me to seek Your ways and to discover the
treasure You have given me. Amen.

Attitude Is Everything

Attitude is everything." You've probably heard this before. It's such a popular expression. It's everywhere—on T-shirts, notebooks, and bags. It's popular because it's true. Your happiness and success in school, friendships, activities, and life in general all starts with your attitude.

School is a terrific example of this. You can make your time there whatever you want it to be. For instance, you can choose for your school experience to be fun and exciting. Or you can decide that school is awful, boring, and the worst nightmare ever. *You* get to make the choice here! And your attitude is contagious. If your attitude shows that something is meaningful and fun, others will pick up on that. Yes, attitude *is* everything!

Jesus, I realize You want me to approach life
with a right attitude. Help me to be excited
about You and the life You've given me—and to
pass on my positive attitude to others! Amen.

Be All There

I have a favorite quote I want to share with you: "Wherever you are, be all there." *Well*, you might be thinking, *of course I'm going to be where I am!* But think about this a little more. If you're at soccer practice, your body needs to be there on the field. And other parts of you need to be there too—your mind, concentrating on the game and what everyone around you is doing; your heart, running your fastest and trying your best; your emotions, not getting discouraged or upset. You need to *be all there!*

It's the same with everything else—"whatever you do, work at it with all your heart, as working for the Lord, not for men" (Colossians 3:23). So when you play soccer, play for the Lord. Do your math for the Lord. Sing in the choir for the Lord. He's your top fan, and He'll always be *all* there for you, cheering you on!

Jesus, I want to live my life full-out for You— to "be all there" no matter where I am. Thank You that You are always right here with me, cheering me on and loving me. Amen.

My Job

Homework. It's something I'll never forget doing! And it seems that the more you have going on in your life, the more homework you have. The week that's packed with music lessons, soccer practice, and your favorite cousin's visit is often the same week your teacher piles on the homework! But your schoolwork *is* important, and you need to make it a top priority. In fact, your main "job" right now is to learn and grow as a student—and God expects you to give it your best.

Are you taking schoolwork seriously? Do you make an effort to do it to the best of your ability? Do you set aside time so you can buckle down and focus? If the answer to any of these questions is no, please do a heart check regarding your priorities—and pray that God will help you become the best student you can be.

Lord, I know I need to make schoolwork a
priority in my life because that's my main job as
a student. Thank You for the gift of an education.
Please help me to take it seriously. Amen.

The Right Start

Getting started on a task is the hardest part of it. That's for sure! And the bigger the task—writing a long paper, studying for a math test, cleaning your messy closet—the more difficult it is to begin. You paint your nails, read magazines, fix yourself a snack... while your task waits and waits and waits!

God gives us a hint on how to get started and how to have a right attitude: "Make every effort to add to your faith goodness; and to goodness, knowledge; and to knowledge, self-control; and to self-control, perseverance" (2 Peter 1:5-6). Wow—that's quite a lot to do...and to remember! But the starting point is faith—faith in the Lord, faith that He will get you started and keep you from getting distracted as you work.

> Lord, there always seem to be so many other exciting things to do when I need to take care of something really important—but not as much fun! Teach me the meaning of the word perseverance. And please help me develop this quality in my life. Amen.

Organize for Success

School is a place for learning. And to learn well, you need to be organized. One thing that helps you get organized is setting up a special place for doing your schoolwork—to organize for success. Ask your parents to help you think of a good place—one that's quiet, free of noise and interruptions, and comfortable enough that you can do your work well.

A fun part of getting organized is all the little stuff you can add to your special space—scented pencils, colorful pens, crazy erasers. Another great addition is a cute timer so you can play "race the clock" and get inspired to finish your homework by a certain time.

Learn to get organized for success in all that you do, and you'll be rewarded!

Jesus, thank You that even something as simple as organizing my space and my stuff can be fun. Even though I have chores and assignments to do, help me to make these things more enjoyable. Amen.

Sooner Is Better

Have you ever had a long time to get something done—so long that you figured you had plenty of time to do it, and then all of a sudden it was almost due? Where did that time go? How did those weeks fly by with that paper still unfinished? How did those weekends pass by without working on that big project?

Here's a big hint—sooner is better! Do your homework or chores first. *Then* do crafts, read a book, or hang out with your friends. It really helps if you set aside a consistent time or place to get your homework and chores done. It helps a lot!

Here's another hint—when it comes to spending time with the Lord, once again, sooner is better! Make time every day for praying to God and reading the Bible—and do it soon!

Lord, I know I can be lazy and put things
off. Sometimes I even put off spending time
with You. Help me to be more disciplined
about getting things done. Help me
remember that sooner is better! Amen.

Certain Place, Certain Time

I'm a writer. So far I've written almost 60 books. How in the world did this happen? It happened because every day I go to my desk (where all my favorite things are) at a certain time. Then I stay there until I write five pages. My best friend, Judy, is an artist. So far she has painted about 100 pictures for gift and children's books. How did this happen? Every day, Judy goes to her work space (where all her neat art supplies are) at a certain time. Then she stays there until she has done her work for the day.

My friend, I will tell you that the years and years—and years!—of doing chores and schoolwork in a certain place, at a certain time, prepared both Judy and me for the work that God has called us to do now—work that we both love.

God has special "work" for you to do, too. Remember—certain place, certain time!

Jesus, You have terrific plans for my future.
I want to jump ahead and see what they
are, but I know that right now I need to
learn the habit of completing my work—in
a certain place, at a certain time. Amen.

Finding Your Thing

It's easy to feel like everyone is good at something, except you. Your sister is a beautiful dancer...but you have two left feet. Your brother is brilliant at chess...but you still can't figure out which way the pieces move. Your best friend's drawings win art contests...but yours look like, well, scribbles. You know that God has given everyone gifts and talents, but yours seem to be hidden under lock and key!

Did you know that even Jesus had to grow and learn how to do things? Luke 2:52 says, "Jesus grew in wisdom and stature, and in favor with God and men." So take heart. God *has* given you some great creative skills and natural talents. With your parents' help and permission, try doing different things until you find your thing, what you're good at. God will lead you to discover it!

Lord, sometimes it feels like everyone is
good at something, except me. Yet I know
that You have given me some amazing
gifts and talents. Help me to discover them,
and to use them for Your glory. Amen.

Listen and Learn

Don't you just love stories that tell what life was like long ago? Maybe you get lost in books about pioneer days. Perhaps you're a big fan of historical novels. You might enjoy learning about Greek and Roman times, or what things were like in Jesus' day. Reading about the past is kind of like time travel—all the fun, but none of the problems!

God uses the gift of stories to tell people more about Him. So look for some of these stories. You'll discover amazing things. Books about missionaries are an excellent place to start. Your parents and grandparents also are a great source of wonderful stories. Ask them about what life was like when they were your age, and how they came to know Jesus. And don't forget the best story ever written—the Bible! Listen...and learn.

God, I love hearing about what life used to be like
and imagining myself in those days. As I read and
learn and hear stories, show me the lessons You
are sharing with me through the words. Amen.

Catching a Glimpse

I'm pretty sure you've looked out a window some-
where at some time into a vast ocean of fog. You
know there are houses across the street or trees up on
the hill, but you can't see beyond the road or drive-
way. Life can be like that. Some days are so busy with
homework and friends and church activities that you
lose sight of what else is out there.

Well, look hard through the fog around your life.
When you do, you'll catch a glimpse of God's great
plan for you. As a girl after God's own heart, your relationship with Jesus is the most important thing *ever*
in your life. This doesn't mean that other things don't
deserve your attention. They do. And Jesus wants
you to work hard, learning and growing to the best
of your ability. Just be sure you are also taking care
of your walk with the Lord. That will help you to see
through the fog of life.

Jesus, thank You for this promise: "The LORD
gives wisdom, and from his mouth come
knowledge and understanding" (Proverbs
2:6). Let me see through the fog of my busy
days as I take time to walk with You. Amen.

Who's Your Crowd?

Some girls think they have it made once they've found their way into the cool-girl crowd. Now that they're a "somebody," they think everything will finally be perfect. Well...not quite! The problem with cool-girl crowds is that those who aren't in them are seen as uncool. So the cool girls avoid the uncool ones—even if they used to be great friends!

Another problem is that those in the cool-girl crowd usually think of themselves as better than everyone else—so they can get pretty mean. As a follower of Christ, you should feel uncomfortable with that. You need to stay apart from such behavior, even if it means rejection from the cool-girl crowd.

Who's your crowd? Would Jesus be proud to have you in it? Would He be a part of it?

God, I want to be accepted and included, but not if it means giving up my real friends or being mean to others. Show me where I can fit in without hurting others. And thank You that everyone is "in" in Your crowd! Amen.

Your Best Friend

Friends. Sometimes it seems like you can't live *with* them, and sometimes it seems like you can't live *without* them! Friends make your life richer, and spending time together helps you grow in your "people skills." Friends also help you develop character as you learn what it means to tell the truth, not spread rumors, and be loyal.

Some girls stress out about having a best friend—someone who will always be there, no matter what. But this doesn't always work out. Best friends can move. Or change all of a sudden. Or just slowly grow apart from each other. That's why it's important to know who your truest friend is—Jesus. He will never move or change or drift away. He always speaks words of kindness, and He's as loyal as loyal can be. What a terrific best friend!

Jesus, thank You for being my best friend.
When I find my friendships changing and
shifting, it helps me so much to know
that You're always there for me. Amen.

Staying Close

Most girls have experienced the pain of a close friend moving away. Maybe she didn't move to another city or state or country, but you no longer attend the same school or church. When you're used to always being together, it takes some effort to stay close and connected when there's now distance between you. Yet God puts good friends in your life for a reason, and you can still keep your friendship strong!

So make sure you and your friend stay in touch. Talk on the phone and e-mail each other. If possible, get together to share and read the Bible and pray. Write notes to each other, and create small gifts for each other. You can even make matching scrapbooks with all your favorite photos. And keep Proverbs 17:17 close to your heart: "A friend loves at all times, and... is born for adversity." Thank the Lord for friends!

Lord, it's hard when a friend moves away or
starts attending another school or church. Help
us stay connected, stay close. Thank You for
the gift of tried-and-true friends. Amen.

Say No to Cliques

You know what a clique is, don't you? It's an exclusive group of people who spend all their time together and don't allow others to join them. At school or even at church, these are the girls who sit together, walk together, talk to each other, and generally have nothing to do with anyone else. Sometimes they even *look* like each other!

Now, there's nothing wrong with having a group of friends that share things in common. The problem comes when the group becomes closed and mean and believes they are better than outsiders. Is this the kind of group you want to be a part of? I hope not.

Cliques consider some people to be nobodies, but in Christ we are all somebodies. So say no to cliques and yes to Jesus!

God, I know that being in a clique is not part
of Your plan for loving others. Help me avoid
the wrong attitudes that can hurt people. Open
my heart to love others the way You do. Amen.

You Are Somebody!

Even though you can be friendly to every single person you meet, that doesn't mean they will be friendly back. Just think of Jesus. He was a friend to all, yet He was criticized because He hung out with the "wrong" people—those who were "sinners" or rejected by others. How did He deal with that?

- He stayed connected to God, and attracted people who wanted to be more like Him.

- He prayed for those who treated Him badly.

- He showed love and kindness to everyone.

As you grow more like Jesus, you won't mind being treated badly so much. You'll attract other girls who want to be more like Jesus. Don't ever forget, you are a "somebody" to Jesus!

Lord, it's sad that some people thought You were a nobody when in fact You were the greatest Somebody of all! Thank You that I am a "somebody" to You. Amen.

Who Are You?

Although you were born to be a one-of-a-kind person, a lot of things influence who you become. For instance, you inherit many traits from your parents and ancestors—the color of your eyes, your height, even some aspects of your personality. You are also influenced greatly by the people you spend your time with. You become what they are.

So who are you? And who do you want to be? Ask yourself these questions as you look for friends. The Bible is very clear about what makes—and doesn't make—a good friend: "He who walks with the wise grows wise, but a companion of fools suffers harm" (Proverbs 13:20). Be sure you seek out friends who are headed in the right direction spiritually—toward Jesus. Hold out for friends who will pull you up in your love for Him.

Jesus, my friends are a huge influence
in my life. Help me to choose them wisely.
I want to walk with the wise and not be
a companion of fools. Lead me to friends
who share my love for You. Amen.

The Ten Commandments
of Friendship

1. Speak to people—there is nothing as nice as a cheerful word of greeting.
2. Smile at people—it takes seventy-two muscles to frown and only fourteen to smile!
3. Call people by name—the sweetest music to anyone's ear is the sound of their own name.
4. Be friendly and helpful—if you would have friends, be friendly.
5. Be cordial—speak and act as if everything you do were a real pleasure.
6. Be genuinely interested in people—you can like everyone if you try.
7. Be generous with praise—cautious with criticism.
8. Be considerate of the feelings of others—it will be appreciated.
9. Be thoughtful of the opinions of others.
10. Be alert to give service—what counts most in life is what we do for others![1]

God, sometimes it's risky to reach out to a potential friend. Please give me the courage to try. Thank You that You always accept me. Amen.

The Golden Rule

You've probably heard some version of the Golden Rule from your parents and teachers: "Do to others as you would have them do to you." Did you know that Jesus taught this rule (see Luke 6:31)? He knew the world would work much better if people treated others the way they wanted to be treated.

The Bible doesn't just tell you to be nice, though. You need to go one step farther: "Be kind and compassionate to one another" (Ephesians 4:32). When you show kindness, you put others first. When you show compassion, you put yourself in someone's shoes and imagine what life is like for them—and then you act on what you feel.

God expects you to forget about your own wants and needs as you focus on Him and others. It's the Golden Rule!

*Jesus, thank You that when I follow Your
rules for living, the world is a better
place. Fix my eyes on You and others as
I live out Your Golden Rule. Amen.*

Better to Be Kind

Believe it or not, there's something better than being nice. God tells us it's better to be kind. If you're nice, you're polite, and that's good. But being kind is being caring and thoughtful. Now, think about how you might want to treat someone who has been mean to you. Is it easy to "act" nice and polite to her even when your inside feelings are different? You can probably do that. But what about showing real care and true thoughtfulness to her? That's nearly impossible!

The Bible says you are to show kindness to everyone: "Love is patient, love is kind" (1 Corinthians 13:4). Being kind takes lots of prayer and effort. It comes from your heart, and it's not just words—it's actions that make a difference. Showing kindness to someone can help point them to Jesus.

Lord, the world tells me to be nice, but I'd rather be like You and be kind. Open my heart. Help me understand other people and show them Your kind of love and compassion. Amen.

No Gossips!

It's been said that the number one enemy of friendships is gossip. So, how do you know when you're gossiping? Well, you talk to your friends all the time—and some of this talk is probably *about* other people. While it's not wrong to talk about others, it *is* wrong if you're saying things that aren't true, or spreading rumors, or sharing secrets that should be kept private. The Bible says a lot about gossip and how it harms friendships: "Whoever spreads slander is a fool" (Proverbs 10:18). And listen to this one: "A talebearer reveals secrets, but he who is of a faithful spirit conceals a matter" (Proverbs 11:13 NKJV).

On the flip side, don't listen to gossip. When someone says something like, "I probably shouldn't be telling you this..."—stop them! You don't want to be a part of betraying a friend. Stay loyal, trustworthy, and truehearted—don't gossip!

God, it's sooo easy to get caught up in gossip! Help me to be more aware of gossip so that it has no place in my life. I want to be a truehearted friend. Amen.

Share Jesus

If you have a personal relationship with Jesus, you have a friend in Him. He is the best friend you could ever have and *will* ever have. He said, "I no longer call you servants...Instead, I have called you friends, for everything that I learned from my Father I have made known to you" (John 15:15). Jesus calls you His *friend*. How cool is that!

Because Jesus is the absolute best friend any girl could ever have, you want to tell others about Him, don't you? But how? You can start by writing out what Jesus means to you—why you believe in Him, how He helps you in times of need. Then pray for a chance to talk to others about Jesus. The best way to start is by sharing about how Christ has helped you. Friends share, so share what matters most to you. Share Jesus.

Jesus, I want to share You with my friends, but
sometimes it's hard to know what to say. Give
me opportunities to tell others about what
You've done in my life and how You're helping
me become a girl after Your own heart. Amen.

The Right Kind of Friend

When you were little, did your parents set up playdates for you with girls from your preschool, your dance class, or friends you met at the library or church? Chances are, first your moms connected and realized they wanted to be friends. Then the moms decided to get the kids together to play. How simple was that!

Now that you're getting older, though, you, along with your parents, are taking part in choosing your friends. You decide who you eat lunch with at school. You choose who to invite home after school. And you decide who comes to your birthday party. These are important choices! Remember, your friends have a tremendous influence on your life. So as you go about the business of choosing your friends, start with prayer!

*God, help me to choose the right kind of friends.
I want to be surrounded by girls after Your
heart, girls who enjoy the adventure of living
for Jesus, girls who will support me spiritually
and encourage me to make good choices. Amen.*

A Prayer for Friends

We've been chatting a lot about friendships. That's important because the people you choose as friends will have a big impact on who *you* become in the future! Here's a special prayer for friends I'd like to share with you right now—

> *Dear Lord, bring friends into my life who will
> love and encourage me, who will bring joy and
> laughter in the good times and comfort and
> support through the bad. Grant me wisdom
> as I seek true friends. I ask that You fill my life
> with real and caring relationships. Amen!*

Whenever you're feeling discouraged in the friendship department, pray this prayer. God will enjoy answering it!

> *God, friends are important, and I know You
> want me to pray about all things. Help me
> to choose friends carefully and to trust Your
> guidance when it comes to friends. Amen.*

A Good Place to Be

on't you love sleeping in once in a while? When you're used to getting up early for school every day, spending a lazy morning in bed is a treat. But when Sundays roll around and you're tempted to skip church, don't. Do whatever it takes to wake up—splash your face with cold water, turn on some music, promise yourself a cup of hot cocoa with whipped cream. Sunday is a day to celebrate!

Sunday is church day, and church is a great place to be. At church, you and your family gather together to worship God. You get to meet with your friends in Bible class. You learn about Jesus and becoming a girl after God's own heart. So refuse to hit the snooze button—get up and get moving! God wants you in church—hearing His Word, learning about Him, and discovering how He wants you to live.

Lord, sometimes it's hard to wake up on
Sunday! But I know it's important to get up
and worship You with other Christians. Thank
You for church—and Sundays! Amen.

God's Plan

You have such an amazing God who did an incredible job of creating you and your world! He has a plan for you—and a plan for all of creation. Part of His plan involves a group of people coming together to worship Him—the church.

Is church a building? No way! You can have church *in* a building, but you can also have church at a campground, on the beach, or in your backyard. Church is God's people coming together to proclaim Christ as Lord and to worship Him with prayer, singing, praise, and Bible teaching. The church is incredibly important to Jesus: "Christ loved the church and gave himself up for her" (Ephesians 5:25). It's the whole reason He came to this earth and gave His life. Thank God for His wonderful plan!

Jesus, it's easy to think of church as a building.
But a church is really the people who are
in it—and I am part of the people who
believe in You as their Lord. Thank You for
giving me a place to worship You! Amen.

Church Isn't Boring!

It's awful when you catch your mind wandering during church or Sunday school, isn't it? You're really trying to pay attention, but you're distracted, or you're even falling asleep a little bit. Oh, dear! You want to learn about Jesus, but you're having a hard time of it.

Church isn't supposed to be boring. The Bible says, "Worship the LORD with gladness; come before him with joyful songs...Enter his gates with thanksgiving and his courts with praise; give thanks to him and praise his name" (Psalm 100:2 and 4). Wow—that sure doesn't sound boring! So get involved. Before church starts, pray that you will pay attention. Participate in the discussion. If a Bible lesson was assigned in advance, be sure to complete it. When you attend church with an eager and open heart, you bring glory to God and grow more like Jesus.

> *Jesus, I confess sometimes I find church a
> bit boring. Please help me to change my
> heart and have a positive attitude about it.
> Help me to get more involved, to be excited
> about all I am being taught. Amen.*

Get Active!

I f you want to become a better runner, you run. If you want to become a better painter, you paint. If you want to become a better piano player, you play the piano. And if you want to become better at living for Jesus, you live for Jesus! The key to improving in anything is doing it over and over and over again. You get active!

You live for Jesus by praying and reading the Bible and attending church, and also by getting involved in youth activities designed for girls your age. Most churches have Bible clubs where you can play games, memorize Scripture, and talk about Jesus with other kids. Some even offer camping trips and retreats.

So get active. Get involved! The things you do and learn will become some of the most important and memorable moments of your entire life. And, as a bonus, you'll make some great friends.

*Jesus, help me to get active and enjoy
all the great activities that are available
to me. I want to live for You. Amen.*

Alone Time

Jesus spent a lot of time with people. He taught the multitudes about His Father, hung out with the disciples, and talked to people one-on-one. Yet He also knew the importance of time alone with God: "Come with me by yourselves to a quiet place" (Mark 6:31). This verse talks about Jesus spending time alone with His disciples, but it can also serve as inspiration for us to spend quiet time with the Lord, too.

Where can you find this "quiet place"? Maybe you have a special area in your room you can retreat to with your Bible, a journal, and a pen. Or perhaps there's a place in your backyard where you can spend time with God. It doesn't really matter *where* your place is. It just matters that you take time to learn from God and talk to Him from your heart and tell Him what's going on in your life.

Lord, I love to spend time with people, but
I know that You also want me to have alone
time with You. Help me find a special place
where I can talk with You every day and
share what's happening in my life. Amen.

All Equal

By now you're used to being ranked and graded in life. Math classes are grouped by ability. Gymnasts and other athletes are divided up into levels. Only one person can be first chair in the band, with everyone else after him or her. But there's one place where everyone is equal. As I've heard all my life, "The ground is level at the foot of the cross." In other words, in Christ, we are all one, all equal and the same. The Bible says, "There is neither Jew nor Greek, slave nor free, male nor female, for you are all one in Christ" (Galatians 3:28).

I hope you're as excited about this promise as I am. What a relief to know God loves all His children—including *you*—the same. He doesn't love some more than others. He doesn't have an elite club for those who read the Bible more or pray more. He loves equally!

God, I am so grateful that the Christian
life isn't a contest to see who can do the
most for You. Thank You that I, like all Your
followers, am beautiful in Your eyes. Amen.

Reaching Out

The best way to get to know a new person is to walk up to her and start talking to her! This comes easily to some people, and is more difficult for others. Jesus spent His life reaching out to people, and He wants you to do the same. If you find it hard to take that first step, ask Him to help you. Here are some ideas for getting started:

- Say hi to everyone—and smile.
- Sit by any girl who is alone. If you're with a friend, both of you can go sit with her.
- If someone is new or a visitor, say hello and be friendly. Ask her where she lives or who she's visiting.

Once you take the first step, you'll discover that reaching out to others is actually a lot of fun!

Jesus, being the first to say hello and introduce myself is kind of scary! Give me the courage to reach out, and put the right words in my mouth. Thank You! Amen.

Church Is About Jesus

How is going to church different from going to school or basketball practice? School and practice both involve lots of people in a joint effort to reach a goal. Church is where you meet with other believers who are learning more about Jesus and growing in His ways.

The main purpose of church is to gather together with others who want to follow Christ, learn more about living for Him, and then *do* it! In church you'll study about Jesus' amazing love—and then you can share this good news with others. You'll find out how the Lord expects you to act and behave—and then you can put His advice into practice. You'll discover that Jesus died for you and your sins—and then you can live for others, loving and forgiving them. Jesus is what church is all about!

> *Lord, help me to see church not as "God class" or "God practice" but instead as a group of people who want to live for You. Help me to live out the things I learn in church when I'm not in church. Amen.*

The Most Important Decision

The most important decision you will ever make is whether you will follow Jesus and give Him your heart and life. You'll never make a decision greater than this one! Where you go to college, whom you marry, what career you choose—these are nothing in comparison.

Jesus makes it very clear how you make this decision. He states, "I am the way and the truth and the life. No one comes to the Father except through me" (John 14:6). It is my prayer that God will use His Word to open your heart to the truth of Jesus' great love for you. I pray that you will respond to His invitation to "come to the Father" and begin to live your life as a girl after God's own heart. Again, no decision is—or ever will be—more important!

Jesus, if I haven't already made a decision for You, open my heart to accept Your love and Your Word. Allow my decision for You to guide all the other decisions in my life as I live as a girl after Your own heart. Amen.

A Heart That Serves

I hope that your career goal is to be a servant. *What?!* You don't *want* to be a servant? Well, I'm not talking about the kind of servant you find in books, like the girl Sarah in *A Little Princess*. I'm talking about a different kind of servant. Did you know Jesus was a servant? "The Son of Man did not come to be served, but to serve, and to give his life as a ransom for many" (Mark 10:45).

There are thousands of ways to be a servant. Whenever you help someone else, you're being a servant. If cupcakes are needed for your class at school, ask your mom if she can help you bake some. If help is needed taking care of toddlers in your church, see if you can volunteer. If an elderly neighbor needs help taking care of her garden, ask if you can do it. By growing a heart that serves, you become a girl who is more like Jesus!

Jesus, the Bible says that You came to serve others. That's what I want too. Open my eyes—and my heart—and show me ways I can serve others in my world. Amen.

Set Apart

You've probably heard the expression "Be *in* the world, but not *of* the world." What does it mean? Well, let's start with being *in* the world. Of course you're in the world—living in your house, on your street, in your city. So yes, you're definitely in this world!

But when you hear God's warning to not be *of* the world, you need to listen up. All around you are negative influences that can draw you away from God. Music with ungodly lyrics, movies that make evil look okay, books that put down parents and authority figures and even God—these are things we want to avoid. Spend your time listening to positive music, reading uplifting books, hanging out with people who are focused on Jesus. Sure, you can live in the world—just don't let it change you!

God, I'm bombarded every day with music and words and messages that don't honor You. It's tempting to get involved in these things, to want to be more like everyone else. Please help me to set myself apart as a girl who lives for You. Amen.

Draw Them In

Just because someone goes to church doesn't mean they're a Christian—even though they might say they are. And just because someone says they don't believe in God doesn't mean they're bad. For sure, it can be confusing to see a mean girl who goes to church...or a nice girl who doesn't believe in God. What are you to make of this?

First, remember that God created each person differently. Some people are nice not because they know Jesus, but because that's just their personality.

Next, remember that God puts people into your life for a reason. He wants you to help point others to Him, to draw them in. So don't be afraid to invite a friend who's not a Christian to a church activity. And don't forget to show kindness to that mean girl in church. God can do anything—including change a person's heart!

*Jesus, it's confusing when those who claim to
follow You act mean and those who say they
don't believe in You are nice. Work through me
so that my life may draw others to You. Amen.*

My Complicated Life

Doesn't it seem like every year your life gets more and more complicated? Eek! So many changes—in your friendships, your schoolwork, your interests, your body, and your dreams. As your friends grow and change too, real friendships get more difficult. Sometimes these changes are hard and you wish that for once something would just stay the same!

Take heart—there *is* one thing in your life that will always be the same, that will never be frustrating or impossible to figure out. That one thing is God Himself. Now, that's not to say God will never allow challenges in your life. He'll do that—but He *Himself* never changes. Never has, never will. You can take comfort in that promise no matter how complicated life gets.

God, sometimes I wish everything in my life would just slow down! All these changes in my body, my moods, my friendships...it's so complicated! Thank You that You are the same yesterday, today, and tomorrow, and that Your love for me never changes. Amen.

Changes!

Sometimes growing up is lots of fun. There are many new things to do almost every day. And as you grow physically, guess what? You need new clothes—and that means s-h-o-p-p-i-n-g! Then there are cell phones and babysitting and all those other cool things that come with getting older. Yes, growing up can be a blast!

But growing up can also be scary as your body changes—sometimes slowly, sometimes quickly—and your responsibilities increase. Thankfully, no matter what happens, God's Word offers all the help and sweet encouragement you need as you adventure through life—and changes—with Jesus. So turn to your Bible when the changes get to be too much, and take comfort in the best book ever written—a book that never changes.

Jesus, growing up is both fun and scary. One minute I'm excited and can't wait for the next thing, and the next I wish I could be a little kid again! But I trust that You are growing me up in the way You want me to go, into a girl after Your heart. Amen.

Soak in God's Love

Bubble baths are the best! You fill the tub with water as hot as you can stand, then pour in a few capfuls of yummy-scented bubble solution. Finally, you grab a favorite book or magazine, maybe get your music going, and then climb into the bathtub, sighing with contentment as you relax in the warm water for a good soak. No matter what's going on in your life, all your cares and worries fade away as the bubbles float around you.

God's love is like a bubble bath—you can always soak in it, relax in its warmth, and let it renew you. God has said, "Never will I leave you; never will I forsake you" (Hebrews 13:5). When you're having one of those days when you feel like you're not very special, God still promises that you are important. You're His princess, and you are greatly loved by Him. That's something you can soak in!

Jesus, thank You that You love me so much!
I want to soak in the fact of Your love and
let You pamper me with it. Renew my heart
so that I can get back out there in the world
and share Your love with others. Amen.

Start with Thanks

You already know that a delicious, healthy breakfast is the best way to start your day, right? Well, it's *almost* the best way. What's really best is to start by thanking God each new morning for His love for you. Do you realize there is never a minute in your life when you are not special to God and loved by Him? He made you. He knows everything about you. And He loves you—no matter what.

So start your day with a breakfast of giving thanks! Pour yourself a big glass of refreshing prayer. Munch down on His inspiring Word. Have a second helping of giving thanks, and wash it all down with some praise! God created you to do something special today. Ask Him what it is, and then keep your heart and mind nourished by God for the rest of your day.

God, I know how important it is not to skip
breakfast. I also know I should start my
day with You through prayer, hearing Your
Word, and listening to Your thoughts. Keep
me nourished every morning. Amen.

This Is the Day!

When I was a brand-new Christian, I found Psalm 118:24 to be incredibly inspiring: "This is the day the LORD has made; let us rejoice and be glad in it." A favorite Sunday school song includes these words, and it's a good one to get stuck in your head! As I read this verse over and over and thought about it, I decided that, before I got out of bed each morning, I would begin the day with these words.

You see, I had a bad habit of not welcoming each new day. As soon as my alarm clock went off, I would make all sorts of excuses about why I didn't want to get up. I was too tired. There was too much to do. I dreaded one thing or another. But then I would remember my decision to greet each new day with joy. And I would say this verse in my heart—even out loud—no matter how I felt: *This is the day the LORD has made; let us rejoice and be glad in it.*

Lord, I want to greet my days with joy!
Remind me to begin each day rejoicing
and thinking of You. Amen.

God's in Control

Have you ever had one of those days that just felt out of control? Maybe you're freaked out about a big test because you haven't had enough time to study. Or you've been hit with the flu and it seems like you'll never get better. Or you're headed to the orthodontist to get braces—you've heard they hurt, and you have no idea what else to expect!

I so clearly remember that out-of-control feeling from my girlhood. I often felt like I wasn't as pretty or cute or clever as some of the other girls. There were days I felt dumb or I was filled with dread. When that happened, it helped to know that Someone was in control of my day and my situation.

So take heart! God is watching over your out-of-control day. He's in control, and He will take care of you.

God, there are so many things I dread—from worrying about math tests to wondering if anyone will play with me at recess. Help me to remember You are in control of my day, so I don't have anything to fear. Amen.

Happiness vs. Joy

There's a difference between happiness and joy. Happiness is an emotion, a right-at-this-moment feeling. And lots of things can make us happy—getting an A+ on a test, scoring a goal in a soccer game, eating ice cream. But happiness doesn't necessarily last. You get a C on the next test. You end up losing the soccer game. And you run out of ice cream.

Joy, however, *does* last. Galatians 5:22 says, "The fruit of the Spirit is...joy." It's a result of having Jesus in your heart. No matter how hard your day is, at the end of it you still have Jesus—and joy. You know that He gives you tomorrow as a new beginning, that He can heal your hurts and make you feel better. You may be down, but you're never out. God's love for you is a forever love, and He will take care of you.

Lord, I love the things that make me happy, but I know there's a greater goal than happiness. Thank You for the lasting joy that comes from placing my trust in You each and every day. Amen.

Mirror, Mirror

Think about this "what if." What if there were a timer hidden inside your mirror that recorded how much time you spend looking at yourself? What do you think the total number of minutes—or hours!—would come to each day? And here's another question: What do you see when you look at your reflection in the mirror?

When most girls look into a mirror, they immediately see everything that's wrong—or that they *think* is wrong! And they completely miss their good features! While it might be impossible to escape mirrors, here's one thing you *can* do: You can look in the mirror less often. Focus on using it simply to make sure your appearance is neat and sends the message that you are a girl after God's own heart—innocent, modest, pure, and sweet.

Jesus, mirrors seem to be everywhere! And
every time I look into one, I find myself
complaining about what's wrong with my
appearance. Help me to see the good in myself
and be realistic about how I should look. Most
of all, help me focus on my heart. Amen.

Look Inside

When you go back-to-school shopping, you visit your favorite stores and try on armloads of clothes, looking for the perfect sizes, colors, and styles. How do you determine what to buy? Well, besides making sure your mom approves of the prices and styles, the clothes need to look good on you!

There are a couple other items that need to look good on you—your heart and your character. The Bible says, "Man looks at the outward appearance, but the LORD looks at the heart" (1 Samuel 16:7). Are you more concerned about your new school wardrobe or what you look like on the inside? What the Lord looks for is different from what people look for, and it's way more important. So go shopping for a pure heart and good character. They're free—just talk to God!

Lord, it's fun to go shopping for new clothes.
But I know I should pay way more attention
to the condition of my heart. Help me to
improve my look with Your love. Amen.

The Real You

I love taking quizzes that determine my style, interests, and personality type. It's fun to see who I am—and who my friends are! But did you know the "real" you is even more amazing than any quiz could ever show? You are the object of God's awesome love. You are a trophy of His grace. You are, I hope, a member of the family of God. This is the real you!

No matter how you look or what abilities you have or don't have, you are precious to Jesus. Listen to how the Bible describes the "real" you—you are "fearfully and wonderfully made" (Psalm 139:14). This is how God views you. And this is how He wants you to think of yourself—*fearfully and wonderfully made*. That's better than any quiz result could ever be!

*God, I praise You for making me in Your
image—I am Your treasure and Your trophy!
Whenever I feel like I'm not worth much, remind
me that You never make mistakes. Through
Your eyes, I can see the real me! Amen.*

Beautiful in God's Eyes

Here's a question to ask yourself. Why do you think of yourself so negatively when God is constantly telling you how beautiful you are? Why are you so hard on yourself when God went to such great lengths—the death of His Son Jesus—to shout out and show His love for you? Why do you put yourself down when God says how pleased He is with you?

It's probably because you're used to seeing yourself through the world's eyes. If you were to look at yourself through God's eyes, you'd see something different. You wouldn't see a growing-up girl struggling with braces, oily skin, and awkwardness. You'd see a beloved daughter of the King—a princess with a gorgeous heart and amazing talents and a sensational smile. You'd see all the potential God has given you. Wow!

Jesus, when I'm down on myself, turn my attention to Your Word and what You say about true prettiness. Fill me up with Your love and help me to realize that I am a beautiful daughter of the King. Amen.

Things to Remember

Vocabulary definitions. Math rules. History names and dates. So many things to remember! I know your brain is already crammed with facts and figures. But I want to give you a few more things to remember for the rest of your life. Don't worry, though. You won't be tested on these. And you can always open the book—God's Word—to remind yourself of the answers.

- You are fearfully and wonderfully made—and God never makes mistakes!

- You can be joyful every second of every day—no matter what's happening—because God is with you.

- You are in a constant state of change as you grow. Some of these changes are new, so make sure you talk them over with your mom.

- You are as special as a one-of-a-kind snowflake, one of God's truly marvelous works!

Jesus, no matter what happens in my life, remind me of these truths from Your Word. Show me that I have value in You and through You. Amen.

Free Time

What a day! You've been busy with school, then afterward you had to practice for the school play. After that you went to the mall with your mom to pick out a birthday present for your brother. And finally there was a big pile of homework waiting for you! You fell into bed dog-tired without reading your Bible or even praying. But then you remembered that you had managed to find some time to watch TV, talk on the phone with a friend, and listen to your favorite music.

Even in what seems like an impossibly busy day, you probably have quite a bit of free time available. Those extra minutes are ideal for reading your Bible and talking to God. In fact, the busy days are when you need to listen to His voice the most! Take time each day to do what's most important—get together with Jesus.

Lord, let me look honestly at how I spend my time. Even on a busy day, do I waste some of it without spending time with You? Help me take time to read Your Word and pray every day—especially on busy days! Amen.

Time Is a Treasure

You would never throw away treasures like gold, silver, diamonds, and pearls, would you? As a girl after God's own heart, you shouldn't throw away your days and minutes either. Why? Because they too are riches and treasures!

You may not think very often about the value of your time and what you spend it on. But the Bible says it's wise to realize how precious time is: "Teach us to number our days aright, that we may gain a heart of wisdom" (Psalm 90:12). So learn to value the gift of *today*. Take a risk. Try something you've always wanted to try. Say hello to someone new. Determine that you will spend this day wisely, this day God has given you, that you will do something big for Him.

Lord, thank You for the gift of time and for
each new day. Let me live every moment
realizing how precious these minutes
and hours are. Help me spend my time
doing things that really matter. Amen.

Don't Delay

It's soooo easy to get in the habit of putting off unpleasant tasks. For instance, your mom asks you to clean your room or do your homework, but you tell yourself, "I'll do it later." Or your teacher has warned the class about a big test coming up, but you haven't even started to study. No matter how hard you wish, your messy room, your homework, and that test are not going to simply disappear into thin air!

Rather than put things off, God gives you a better way of getting things done: "I will hasten and not delay to obey your commands" (Psalm 119:60). So block out what you *want* to do and focus on what you *need* to do. Set little goals for yourself—study for 30 minutes, then eat a snack; clean up your desk, then take a break; practice your instrument for 15 minutes, then play with your sister. Don't delay—get it done, and then have fun!

> *Jesus, help me to stop putting things*
> *off and instead, follow Your "don't*
> *delay" rule. I know that by getting things*
> *done, I'll bring honor to You. Amen.*

A Time for Everything

As a busy person, time management is really important to me. One of my favorite Bible verses is all about time: "There is a time for everything, and a season for every activity under heaven" (Ecclesiastes 3:1). I love this verse because it promises I will have time for all those great things that I long to do—that is, if it's God's plan for me to do them.

Sometimes you need to make difficult decisions about what you do and don't do. Maybe you want to join the track club and take a jazz class—but they're at the same time! So you pray, you write down the pros and cons—the good and not-so-good—of each activity, talk to your parents, and then make a choice. Maybe someday you can do both, but right now it just won't work out. Please, don't get discouraged. Trust me—if God wants you to do something, He will open that door at just the right time!

God, let me listen to Your voice and to the advice of my parents as I make decisions about my activities and how I spend my time. Help me use my time wisely. Amen.

Never Be Bored!

You're sitting at home, and it seems like there is absolutely nothing to do! Your friends can't come over, your brother is at a birthday party, your sister is at church camp, you've finished every last bit of your homework, *and* you've completed all your chores. And you're not in the mood to play a game or watch a movie. Suddenly, out of your mouth comes a huge sigh and those two dreadful words—*I'm bored!*

Being bored is...well...boring! Did you know there's a secret to never being bored? It's this: Make a list of "Five Things I Want to Do." You can list goals or dreams, hobbies, books you'd like to read, something new you'd love to know about or learn to do. Then file away that list and pull it out the next time the temptation to say, "I'm bored!" begins to creep over you. God has big plans for your life—and...well, His plans are never boring!

Jesus, it's never fun to be bored! I know I could
use that time to pray or read my Bible or work
on the hopes and dreams You've put in my
heart. Help me put my time to good use. Amen.

You Choose

What can you do with a free afternoon? You could work on writing a book, complete with your own illustrations. You could write to a missionary or a pen pal. You could design and make your own jewelry. You could enjoy time with your doll collection, even sew clothes for the dolls. You could even work on a personal Bible study that's just for you. You choose!

Time is a treasure. It's a gift from God. And He wants you to value each day and use your time well. Your parents and responsibilities determine much of how your time is spent. But anything beyond that is your free time. The better you use it, the greater the rewards will be later. Maybe God is growing something special in your life—and He's giving You free time to develop those gifts and talents. Choose to use it—not waste it.

Lord, teach me the value of using my free time well, using it wisely. Whatever it is I do with my schedule, I want it to glorify You. Amen.

Evaluate Your Priorities

Okay, so you have a big list going of all the things you want to do. You'll never be bored again! But now you have another dilemma. With all the things on that list, how do you choose the *best* one? You may be talented, but you can't read a book, sew a cute bag, and learn sign language all at the same time, can you?

First, take a look at the priorities—the things in your life that you *must* do, that are "set in stone." Many of your activities—like school—have been decided for you by others. Other things, like chores, music lessons, and church activities, have been established for you by your parents. But the rest of your time is yours! As you decide how to use it, remember this advice from God's Word: "Whatever you do, whether in word or deed, do it all in the name of the Lord Jesus" (Colossians 3:17).

> *Jesus, no matter what I'm doing—from cleaning the bathroom to building a tree fort—let me do it in Your name. Help me take care of my priorities before I move on to the fun things I want to do. Amen.*

Plan a Meeting

I f you don't do some planning, time with Jesus can get crowded right out of your life! Now, Jesus doesn't ask you to skip school, ditch family dinners, or put off piano practice in order to spend time with Him. But He does want you to set aside special time for Him, just like you do for homework or friends. He wants you to plan time to meet with Him. This is the most important priority you have every day! Here's what the Bible says about meeting with Jesus and seeking Him:

- ◎ "Seek first his kingdom and his righteousness" (Matthew 6:33).
- ◎ "Blessed [happy] are they who keep his statutes and seek him with all their heart" (Psalm 119:2).
- ◎ "I seek you with all my heart" (Psalm 119:10).

Lord, I know that meeting with You is the most important part of my day. I want to plan to meet with You every day! I want to seek You with all of my heart. Amen.

Make a Commitment

Would you fail to show up for a meeting with a teacher? I don't think so! Would you skip your best friend's birthday party? No way! If you would keep your commitment to these things, I hope you would want to commit to spending time with Jesus, the most important person in the whole world.

Amazing things happen when you spend time with Jesus. He gives you a joyful heart. He helps you do your best. He shows you how to be more kind and helpful to others. And He does His amazing work of transforming you into a girl after His own heart! So make a commitment to spending time with Him. Pray as you walk to school. Read from your Bible before you go to bed. Call a friend and ask her to pray for you—and vice versa. Make Jesus a key part of every day!

Lord, I know how important it is to spend time with You. I want to say yes to reading my Bible, praying, and thinking about Your awesome love and power. Fill my heart with worship as I commit to these things with You. Amen.

J-E-S-U-S

I have a fun little way to remember some key truths about Jesus. I use an *acrostic*—a word in which each letter stands for something. This particular acrostic—which spells **J-E-S-U-S**—is actually a sentence:

> **J**esus, the Son of God,
>
> **E**ntered this world as a baby, and
>
> **S**acrificed Himself for sinners to
>
> **U**nite them with the Father by
>
> **S**ecuring eternal life for all who
> believe in Him.

And why is Jesus so important? He lived *in* this world, so He knows what life here is like. And He took upon Himself all your sins! You should be very grateful for what He did. Let these truths inspire you to become more like Him and to do what He asks of you.

Jesus, You lived and walked in this world, so You know what it's like! Thank You for sacrificing Yourself for my sins and securing eternal life for me. I love You! Amen.

No Matter What

Sometimes when you sit down to pray, you can't think of anything to say. You know you have lots to talk to God about, but your mind just goes blank! At times like this, it's okay to pray prayers from the Bible or from other books. Or you can pray this prayer:

God, I want to be Your child, a girl who lives
her life in You, and through You, and for
You—not for myself. I admit I often fail to do
what You say is right. I thank You that Jesus
died on the cross for my sins. Thank You for
giving me Your grace and Your strength so that
I can follow You with all my heart. Amen.

As you continue on your journey with Jesus, remember that the number one key to staying close to Him is developing a prayerful heart.

Jesus, my desire is to develop my prayer life
as you grow me into a girl after Your own heart.
Even when I don't know what to say, may
I keep on looking to You for guidance. Amen.

Golden Rules for Living

Did you know that making your bed and clearing away your dishes is connected to your spiritual growth as a girl after God's own heart? Having good manners and showing courtesy to others really *does* matter to God! To help you on your journey, here are some "Golden Rules for Living":

- If you open it, close it.
- If you turn it on, turn it off.
- If you break it, admit it.
- If you can't fix it, call in someone who can—like Mom or Dad.
- If you borrow it, return it.
- If you value it, take care of it.
- If you make a mess, clean it up.
- If it belongs to someone else, get permission to use it.

God, help me to be courteous, thoughtful, and giving as I work to improve my manners and think of others. Amen.

Time Fast

Have you ever heard of a fast? That's when you give up food for a certain amount of time in order to focus on God and your spiritual growth. Now, it's not safe for a girl your age to go on this kind of a fast. Your growing body needs nutritious food at regular times throughout the day. But you *can* go on another kind of fast to get closer to God. It's called a time fast.

To do a time fast, choose one thing you will give up for a period of time—watching TV, playing on the computer, going to the mall, talking on the phone. Then spend that time with Jesus. Talk to Him. Read the words in the Bible. Journal what you're learning about Him. And when your fast is over and you get back to your regular activities, keep spending time with the Lord. After all, He's your friend for life!

Jesus, I'm so thankful You're so special to me.
You're my Lord...and my friend. Lead me in
Your ways during my time fast, and when it's
over, let's plan to meet again tomorrow. Amen.

Super Swap

Have you ever swapped a Christmas present for something else? Maybe you received a goofy-looking shirt ten sizes too big and traded it in for a fun one that actually fit. Or you received a book you already own, so you exchanged it for another one. When you spend time with Jesus, you make the best swap of all—your human abilities, which are way too small for the Christian life, for God's amazing strength. When you go to God, you swap...

> your weakness for His power,
>
> your darkness for His light,
>
> your problems for His solutions,
>
> your frustrations for His peace,
>
> your hopes for His promises,
>
> your questions for His answers, and
>
> the impossible for the possible!

*Lord, I have a heart full of things I want
to swap for Your better version. I'm
ready to trade my problems for Your
solutions and Your peace. Amen.*

Keep a List

What girl doesn't like making birthday lists or Christmas lists? And, you can also keep a list of books you'd like to read or things you want to learn how to do. But the best kind of list you can keep is a prayer list. It might start out short, but soon you'll think of more and more needs to bring to God. And then you'll branch out beyond your own needs and write down the needs of friends, family members, and others.

You can also keep a journal of how God answers your prayers. This is a neat way to learn more about God and how He works. You'll see how some prayers are answered right away, while others take a long time. And you'll be surprised by the unexpected ways He might answer! As you see how God answers your prayers, your faith in Him will go sky-high!

God, as I get out my notebook and pen to begin a prayer list right now, let me start with a prayer for my own growth. And as I lift up the needs on my list, keep me focused on learning more about Your love and Your ways. Amen.

Recipe for Faith

Baking looks like a pretty simple process. You look at the recipe, gather the items you need, mix 'em together, pop the whole thing in the oven for a certain number of minutes—and out comes a yummy treat! But if you miss an ingredient—even one single ingredient—what comes out will taste pretty awful. My daughter Katherine once made brownies for the family...and left out the salt. Well, you can imagine how *those* tasted. Forget seconds—nobody wanted firsts!

Just as a batch of brownies requires specific ingredients to become a delicious dessert, several ingredients are needed for *you* to become a girl who loves God with her whole heart. You can love God, love His Word, and love prayer—but if you don't love to obey, the result is going to be a disaster! The complete recipe for faith always includes obeying what God says. So make sure you get the ingredients right!

Jesus, I want to live my life for You.
I want to get the recipe right! Help me
gather all the ingredients I need for a
life of faith. And don't let me forget the
essential ingredient of obedience. Amen.

Stay on the Path

Hiking is so much fun—unless you get lost! One of the surest ways to do that is by venturing off the path. And once you've left the main trail, it can be really hard to find your way back.

Just as you would pack a whistle and water bottle for a hike, you can pack the five C's to staying on the path of your walk with God. **C**oncentrate on doing what is right. Turn to God's Word for direction. **C**ease doing what is wrong. God's strength makes this possible. **C**onfess any sin. Get rid of what holds you back. **C**lear things up with others. Ask for and give forgiveness. **C**ontinue on as soon as possible. Don't get stuck believing you're not worthy of God's love.

And if you wander off the path, you can always count on God to help you find your way back onto His trail...and to forgive you.

God, You are my GPS unit in life! If I have You with me on a hike, I can never possibly get lost. I want to go down Your trail! Amen.

Honestly!

Y ou know it's important to be honest, but you are also tempted to lie. Now, while we're talking about honesty, be honest. Have you ever given in to that temptation and lied? Of course you have! Everyone has at one time or another, whether it's "stretching the truth" or blatantly lying. It grieves God's Spirit when you lie, and it can really destroy your relationships with your parents, friends, teachers, and other people.

God expects you to be up-front and honest about everything—not only with others, but also with yourself. If someone gives you honest correction or advice, keep an open mind. That person is helping you because he or she cares about you. As a girl after God's own heart, it's essential that you be honest with others—and yourself.

God, when I'm tempted to lie, point me
toward Your truth. I know lying can destroy
relationships and that it's really hard to go back
to being truthful after I tell a lie. Help me to be
honest with You, others, and myself. Amen.

Flattery vs. Praise

The Bible warns us not to flatter others, but it can be tricky to tell the difference between flattery and praise. Is it okay to give compliments and talk about others in a positive manner? Yes, the Bible tells us to encourage and build one another up. So, to avoid flattery, be specific with your praise. Instead of telling a teammate, "Good game!" say, "Your passing was right-on today, and you played really tough defense!" Being specific helps you to be honest.

Also ask, "What is my motivation for giving a compliment? Am I being nice in the hopes of getting something back?" If yes, then your "compliment" is flattery. You don't really care about the person. You just care about what she can do for you. Learn to praise honestly and from the heart, with the purpose of building others up. That's true praise!

Jesus, sometimes I'm tempted to say something nice just so others will like me or think good things about me. Teach me how to encourage others honestly in a way that pleases You. Amen.

The Sunday Scene

Here's something new to try: Talk to your friends before Sunday school and agree *not* to sit or visit together while you're at church. Now, why would you want to do this? Your friends are fun to hang out with, right? And you have neat discussions about God and life with them. Well, I'm not saying you should do this *every* week, but think about the Sunday scene for a moment. If you and your friends are always together, you're still limiting yourself from meeting new people and getting to know others better.

You can really grow by spreading out and connecting with others. Introduce yourself to someone who's visiting. Walk up to someone you've rarely talked to, smile, and start talking. You'll discover that your church is overflowing with people just like you who want to connect. So divide up. Go discover some of the great people who make up your church!

Lord, it's easy to get stuck in the routine of sitting with my best friends all the time. Help me think of others and reach out to connect with new people. After all, we're all family! Amen.

Where Are You?

A fun variation of the game Hide and Seek is the game of Sardines. It's like Hide and Seek, but reversed. Instead of a bunch of people hiding and one person finding them all, one person hides and everyone else goes in search of the hidden person. When you find that person, you hide with him or her—until the final person discovers everyone laughing and giggling as they cram into one tight spot.

Life can be like the game of Sardines. If you're the first person who hides, your spot feels pretty roomy and comfortable—until everyone else hides with you! So look around you. Do you like where you are? Are you surrounded by good companions? If so, great! Stay there—and keep growing and playing! If not, then make changes that will help you get to know more friends and allow you to participate in things you enjoy.

Jesus, I know that life isn't a game—it's for real. And I know You want me to enjoy what I do and the friends I have. Please put me in the place where You want me to be. Amen.

Sweet Dreams

When you close your eyes and your head hits the pillow, it's dream time! Did you know you don't have to be sound asleep to dream? You can also dream when you close your eyes and pray. This is the best kind of "dreaming" because the dreams you have as a girl after God's own heart can become reality. Cool, isn't it? If the things you pray for are things God wants you to have, then get ready for Him to make your dreams come true!

Think about the girl you want to be a year from now, and tell God all about it. What do you want to do? Where do you want to be in your walk with Jesus? In what ways do you want to become more like Him?

Your dreams may be sweet, but the way God can make them come true is even sweeter!

God, You are the One who makes my dreams come true. Give me a heart of faith and remind me that it's okay to dream big because You and Your love for me have no limit. Your purpose and plan for my life are dreams waiting to come true! Amen.

Cravings

Do you crave candy bars more than veggies? Be honest! It's pretty hard to turn down something sweet, and the things that are good for us don't always tempt our taste buds. But you already know which things are better for you. And as you walk with God, you'll grow toward making choices that please Him. Step by step, the thoughts you think, the words you say, and the actions you take will focus on what's better for you.

Now, this doesn't mean that tomorrow you'll wake up thinking about carrots instead of chocolate chip cookies! But the closer you walk with Jesus, the more you'll think about your choices—and their consequences. You'll begin to crave the things that are truly good for you, good for others, and good for your world.

Lord, it's hard to turn down the things
that bring me immediate happiness! But I
know they aren't always good for me in the
long run. Lead me to the things that will
nourish me the most to live for You. Amen.

Share the Love

When kids cut in front of you in line at recess, do you hug them? When a girl writes a mean note about you, do you put her first on your prayer list? When your coach finds fault with the way you're playing, do you say, "Thank you"? These aren't your typical responses to being hurt, are they? Yet as a girl after God's own heart, you're supposed to love others as God loves you...and give these kinds of responses.

When you're tired or your feelings have been hurt, you really aren't in the mood to love other people. But Christian love isn't something you feel automatically—it's something you *choose* to show. By God's grace, you can show love when the human part of you doesn't want to. You can help someone even when you're hurting. This kind of love comes only through God. With His strength, you can share the love with others.

God, thank You so much for Your love and grace!
You always love me despite my words and actions.
When I'm sad or upset or tired, fill me with Your
kind of love so I can share it with others. Amen.

Gift of Joy

What makes your day? An invitation to a birthday party? A perfect score on a test? Praise from your parents?

A better question is, do you look to God as the ultimate One who can make your day? There are so many reasons to turn to God, and one is that *He* is the source of lasting joy. So claim His gift of joy—grab hold of it, embrace it, and never let it go! A good way to do this is by picking up a favorite pen and some cute notebook paper and writing out some of God's promises from the Bible on separate slips of paper. Put the slips of paper in a basket and then, every morning, draw out a promise to read and keep with you during the day.

And on the days when you're really struggling, be *especially* sure you reach for one of God's promises. Let it encourage you and give you joy.

Jesus, thank You for Your promises—that
they're gifts from You I can keep, that
they can give me joy no matter what
else is happening in my life! Amen.

Peace, Not Panic!

Pop quiz in school! Home alone and you hear funny noises outside! Best friend absent and nobody to sit by at lunch! Are you quick to hit the panic button? If so, stop. Instead, choose to be filled with God's peace:

- 🌀 choose not to panic...and rest in God's presence,

- 🌀 release your terror...and trust in God's wisdom and ways,

- 🌀 reject your nervousness...and remember God is in control,

- 🌀 ignore your dread...and accept God's dealings.

You'll know Jesus is with you from beginning to end when you choose peace instead of panic!

Lord, You have given me the truths I need to experience peace. Help me remember them. Show me how to use them. Then let me practice, practice, practice so I can know what to do when I want to hit the panic button. Amen.

The Way Home

Have you ever played a game where you're riding in the car with your mom or dad and *you* are in charge of finding the way home? It's a neat way to learn more about where you live and how to get there! At every intersection, you choose which way to go—right, left, or straight. Now, if you give even just *one* wrong direction, you won't make it home.

How are you at following God's directions for your life? Do you know which way to turn when you're at an intersection? Are you noticing the signs He has given to guide you? Or do you wander around, not paying attention, then freak out when you find yourself lost? That's what happens when you try to handle life on your own. Be wise. Turn to your heavenly Father and ask Him for guidance. Then follow those directions until you find your way home.

God, it seems so simple to find my way home, but I can get really lost if I take one wrong turn! Open my eyes to the signs You've given me to guide me. And when I'm lost, let me follow Your directions home. Amen.

Adorning Your Heart

Bracelets, necklaces, earrings, hair clips, and fancy headbands—accessories are tons of fun. But their only purpose is to draw attention to you. What's more important than your clothes and cool add-on bling and jewelry is who you are on the inside! Before you add any accessories and do-dads to your outfits, you need to make sure you're properly dressed on the inside.

What are the basics for a girl after God's own heart's wardrobe? Be sure you clothe yourself first with prayer, with the Word of God, and with God's fruit of the Spirit. Here's what Galatians 5:22-23 says makes up the fruit of the Spirit: "love, joy, peace, patience, kindness, goodness, faithfulness, gentleness, and self-control." After you've adorned your *heart*, then add the extras. Express your personality. Add something that's your favorite color. Choose your favorite pair of tennis shoes—you know, the ones with the glitter! Then step into your wonderful world with a heart that loves God and loves people. What a blessing you will be!

Lord, thank You that Your clothes never go out of style and that they're always there for me to wear. Help me adorn my heart with the fruit of the Spirit, and dress me with Your love. Amen.

Vision Test

You've had your eyes checked before, haven't you? You know the drill. You look at a chart on the wall. Then try to read the letters, first with one eye, then the other. If you can read the chart, great! You're good to go. But if you can't make out the letters, you know you need to get your vision corrected. That means glasses or contacts—which can help you to see things clearly again. Now that's something to celebrate!

When you come to know Christ and begin to see the world and other people through His eyes, that's something to celebrate too! In fact, He fine-tunes all our senses so we see things in a whole new way—His way. You learn to love as God loves, see as God sees, and hear as God hears. As you go about your day, you can look and listen—and then do what God wants you to do!

God, help me to start seeing others as You see them and treating them as You want me to treat them. Work on my heart so that I go about my days with a spirit of love. Amen.

True You

Do you save your best behavior only for church? Are you super nice to your friends...and then treat your parents and siblings with less love? Are you always the first to volunteer to help out at school but slack off on your chores at home? While it's important to do the right thing and live for Christ when you're away from home, keep this in mind: What you are at home is who you *really* are. It's in your own house that your true character comes out.

And did you know that eventually your at-home behavior will start to show in your out-in-public behavior? You can't fake it forever! So live out God's commands at home. Treat your parents and siblings well. Do what you can to make their lives easier and the mood in your house more joyful. Let your best behavior be your all-the-time behavior!

Jesus, help me to show kindness to my family. Remind me to do the little, thoughtful things that show love and respect for my parents and siblings and honor You in my home. Amen.

Choosing Christ

I know girls who are disliked at school because they live for Jesus. But in their hearts they determine, "I'm going to respond in goodness to whatever mean things girls say about me. I want to be a good advertisement for Christ!"

Other girls I know are hurt right in their own church by the Christians in their youth group. Here's how they deal with this: "I choose not to feel hurt when I'm not included in their activities. I choose not to feel bitterness or resentment. I choose to show my love for them."

When people hurt you and you're not sure about what to do, pray, "Lord, what is the right response to this?" Choose to focus on Christ. Choose to act like Christ, and He will give you the strength to face anything!

God, let me respond in love when I encounter hurtful people and mean comments. Let me choose You and the right kind of behavior. Help me answer to hatred with Your love. Amen.

Spiritual Strength

If you're an active girl, you probably have the muscles to show for it! And when you're walking with Jesus and exercising in Him, you develop spiritual strength. This strength becomes visible when you show self-control—God's kind. Here's what it looks like:

- ◎ Self-control controls and checks the self.
- ◎ Self-control restrains the self.
- ◎ Self-control disciplines and masters the self.
- ◎ Self-control says no to self.

Do you struggle with self-control—such as poor food choices, putting off your homework, or leaving your room messy? If so, write the list above on a small card and tape it to your bathroom mirror. Every time you see the list, pray that God will help you with self-control.

God, I want to have the kind of strength
that comes from You. Then, when others
ask me how I got to be so strong, I can
give You the glory and direct them to You
as the source of all strength! Amen.

Heart to Heart

As you talk more and more to the Lord through prayer, you'll realize He's becoming your closest friend. You'll start turning to Him for help with everything that's important to you—your relationship with your family, your changing and growing friendships, your homework and school activities, and everything about your future!

When you pray, you are worshipping God. You are telling Him how much you love Him. You are bringing your needs before Him. It's a back-and-forth conversation—you not only talk to God, you spend time listening to Him too. These precious talks with the Lord will be the most incredible conversations *of* your life *for* your life. What an amazing experience—you and the God of the universe talking to each other one-on-one and heart-to-heart!

Jesus, I love talking to my friends about
anything and everything—but most of all,
I love having heart-to-heart talks with You!
I know that taking time to pray will help me
grow as a girl after Your own heart! Amen.

Happy Birthday

On my tenth birthday as a Christian I prayed and thanked God for His mercy, grace, wisdom, and salvation. And then I prayed, "Lord, is there anything missing from my Christian life that I should focus on for the next ten years?" Right away I knew in my heart what the answer was—prayer! That day I opened up a pretty blank journal my daughter had given me and wrote, "I dedicate and purpose to spend the next ten years in the Lord developing a meaningful prayer life."

Whether this is your one-week or one-year birthday in the Lord, ask Him what He wants you to focus on in the days, weeks, and years ahead. Spend time with Him praying for direction in your life. Thank Him for your birthday as a Christian, and enjoy unwrapping the presents He gives you all year long!

*Jesus, birthdays are so fun to celebrate—
especially my birthday of new life and
coming to know You! Show me what You
would like me to focus on in the future. Help
me build a life of prayer and a life lived
as a girl after Your own heart. Amen.*

Prayer Princess

As a girl after God's own heart and a princess in His royal kingdom, prayer is truly the most majestic of all habits you could desire! As a princess with a busy schedule, however, you need to create a few castle rules that will make sure you take time to pray:

- Write down specific times to pray—when you get up in the morning, at lunch, before you go to bed.
- Pray together with a friend each day, either in person or on the phone.
- Start or join a girls' prayer group through your church or youth group.

As you embrace the habit of prayer, God will reward you with the riches of a happy and holy life. The King of kings is waiting to hear your voice!

God, I am so thankful I'm a royal princess
in Your kingdom. As I come to You in prayer,
I enter Your presence with respect and
awe. I bow down at Your throne and
pour out my heart to You. Amen.

Don't Hide!

Do you avoid talking to your parents when you've done something wrong? Do you stay away from a friend after talking about her behind her back? Do you try to act invisible in class so your teacher doesn't find out you didn't complete your assignment? It might be easy to hide for a little while, but at some point you're going to be noticed and the truth will come out.

You're not the only one who's hidden behind your sin. Adam and Eve avoided God after they disobeyed Him. King David stopped praying after he sinned. But hiding your secrets behind silence only traps the sin—and makes it worse. So tell the truth...and then apologize to God and those around you. Say "I'm sorry" and experience the power of God's forgiveness. Then delight in the healing that follows.

> *Lord, when I've done something wrong,*
> *I think that if I keep silent the situation*
> *will just disappear. But that's not true,*
> *for You see and reveal all things. Give*
> *me courage to admit what I've done, and*
> *thank You for Your forgiving love. Amen.*

Turn Your Eyes

ook around. Who...or what...influences you? Are you surrounded by people and things that please God? Or are you drawn to the things of the world? Would you rather read your Bible or a Christian book...or skim through a magazine that glorifies pop stars and what's currently "in"? Do you choose friends who are walking with Jesus...or those who sparkle with the latest style yet make decisions you know aren't okay?

A natural part of growing up is "trying on" different styles and ways of doing things. You're figuring out who you are, and that's important. But through it all, ask yourself if your heart is growing closer to God or drifting away from Him. Which is it? When you turn your eyes to Jesus, the negative influences of the world lose their brilliance. Make sure you keep your focus on Him!

Jesus, as I'm growing up and figuring out who I am, keep my eyes fixed on You. Give me good judgment to choose the things that honor You and to reject the things that pull me away from You. Amen.

Perfect Presents

Look! A surprise package just showed up for you! In it are four perfect presents—four sources of God's peace. Let's unwrap them one by one.

God, the Son—Jesus' work on the cross made possible your relationship and peace with God.

God, the Father—Through the Bible you can learn about God, His promises, and His faithfulness to you.

God's Word—When you follow God's Word and its teachings, you experience the peace that comes from keeping a right relationship with God.

God, the Spirit—John 14:27 reveals the gift of the Holy Spirit: "My peace I give you...Do not let your hearts be troubled." The Holy Spirit gives you peace.

Praise God for His perfect presents—given to you at just the right time, in just the right place!

> *Lord, thank You for Your four unchanging*
> *sources of Your peace. On my own, I mess*
> *up. But with Your help and the peace that*
> *I find in You and Your Word, I am able to*
> *change my worry to worship. Amen.*

Failed Friendship

You've probably had a friendship that started out great, but then something went totally wrong. Maybe your friend suddenly became "too busy" and started avoiding you. Or she said something about you that wasn't true or hurt your feelings. Perhaps she walked away because you weren't "cool" enough for her anymore. Or she simply turned against you for no reason at all.

It's so hard when friendships fail. You're left feeling sad, missing the great times you shared. You never head into a friendship expecting it to end, so when it does, it's natural to feel confused. But people aren't perfect, so it's going to happen sometime in your life. And when it does, you can bring your hurting heart to God. He'll wrap you in His arms and remind you that His love for you will *never* fail.

Lord, it's hard when a friendship ends.
Please help me forgive the person who hurts
me and let me draw strength and comfort
from my friendship with You. Amen.

Just Pray

When something goes wrong during your day, it's nice to know you're not alone. God is always right there for you! And you can talk to Him at any time. Even when you don't know the right words to pray, the Holy Spirit does. He prays with you and for you.

So don't worry about the words—just share your heart with God. When you're hurting, pray. When you're confused, pray. When you're sad, pray. When you're feeling angry or overwhelmed, pray. And when you're not sure what exactly you're feeling...yes, pray!

Are you aware God knows what you need *before* you even ask? So be bold—bring up anything and everything to Him. It doesn't matter what you say—just say it! And let God take care of the rest.

Jesus, I'm amazed You know my thoughts and prayers even before I say them. Sometimes I'm worried that I'm not praying the right way, and it's comforting to know I don't have to worry about that. You just care that I pray! Amen.

Knowing Christ

Even if you've been attending church or Christian school all your life, you might not actually know Christ. Or maybe you're not sure if you have a personal relationship with Him. Here are some good questions to ask yourself: "What does it mean to be a Christian? Am I a Christian? And how can I become a Christian?"

The book of Romans tells how you can become God's child:

The Romans Road

- Romans 3:23 tells you about your sinful condition.

- Romans 6:23 shows you the result of your sinful condition and reveals the gift God offers to you instead.

- Romans 5:8 points out God's grace and love for you and Christ's answer to your sinful condition.

- Romans 10:9-10 reveals how to become a Christian.

I meet girls all the time who are not sure if they are a Christian. Is this something you are wondering? Well, here's how. The way to become a Christian is to receive Jesus Christ as your personal Savior. Read again the verses entitled "The Romans Road." They show you the same key truths about Jesus and how to come to know Him.

God, I want to know Christ. I want to make sure that I am a Christian. If I've never given my life to You, or if I'm not sure, show me what to do. Place people in my life who will help me come to know You and grow in You. Speak to me through Your Word. Amen.

You Did It!

Give yourself a round of applause—you've read this book all the way through! As you think back on all you've experienced and learned and prayed about since starting this devotional, I'm sure you can think of tons of ways you've gotten closer to God. I hope you will go through this book again and again as you continue on your journey to becoming a girl after God's own heart.

But even more important than re-reading these devotions is making the effort to put the things you've learned into practice. After all, practice makes permanent! My prayer is that you'll keep looking to Jesus, talking to God, growing in His ways, and receiving His joy. And as you do, you'll continue to receive His blessings!

Lord, may I spend time every day thinking about You, following Your Word, and delighting in Your work in my life. Help me to love You more, understand You better, and give my life to You completely. Thank You for continuing to teach me more and more about becoming a girl after Your own heart. Amen.

Notes

1. Roy B. Zuck, *The Speaker's Quote Book* (Grand Rapids, MI: Kregel, 1997), p. 159.

WHAT I'M LEARNING

WHAT I'M LEARNING

WHAT I'M LEARNING

WHAT I'M LEARNING

WHAT I'M LEARNING

WHAT I'M LEARNING

_____

_____

_____

_____

_____

_____

_____

_____

_____

_____

_____

_____

_____

_____

_____

_____

_____

_____

WHAT I'M LEARNING

More Books by Elizabeth George

A Girl After God's Own Heart

How can I find a real best friend? How can I get along with my brothers and sisters? How can I make time in my busy life for Jesus? How can I know the right things to say and do—especially when I keep messing up? God is ready to help you, and gives His answers in the Bible. Learn what it means to be a girl after God's own heart—a girl who loves Him and follows Him, and wants to please Him in everything she does.

A Young Woman After God's Own Heart

What does it mean to include God's heart in your everyday life? It means understanding and following His wonderful plan for your friendships, your faith, your family relationships, and your future. Learn how to grow close to God, enjoy meaningful relationships, make wise choices, become spiritually strong, build a better future, and fulfill the desires of your heart.

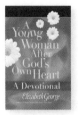

A Young Woman After God's Own Heart—A Devotional

God wants to encourage you each and every day! He has things to say to you that can change your day, take away your worries, and give you joy. In His amazing love, He cares about all the details of your life. In this pocket-sized devotional, you'll learn how to take your problems to God, let go of your anxiety, live your faith, find a real friend in Jesus, and grow in true beauty and confidence.

A Young Woman's Walk with God

Love, joy, peace, patience, kindness, goodness, faithfulness, gentleness, and self-control are qualities Jesus possessed—and He wants you to have them too! Elizabeth George takes you step by step through the fruit of the Spirit to help you get the most out of your life.

A Young Woman's Guide to Making Right Choices

When it comes to making decisions, how can you make sure you are making the right choices, the best choices? Do you desire to please God in the way you pick your friends, spend your time, and treat your family? You'll find useful checkpoints for helping you understand God's wisdom and living it out.

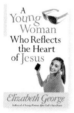

A Young Woman Who Reflects the Heart of Jesus

As you grow up, life gets more exciting, more fun, and more challenging. So much more to do, so many more choices to make. How can you consistently do what is best—and avoid making bad mistakes—at every step of the way? From Jesus you'll learn 12 character qualities that make life so much better. Let Him teach you about being confident, focused, friendly, responsible, thankful, wise, and more.